WORKS AND CRITICISM
of GERARD MANLEY HOPKINS:
A COMPREHENSIVE BIBLIOGRAPHY

BY

EDWARD H. COHEN

THE CATHOLIC UNIVERSITY OF AMERICA PRESS

Washington, D. C.

1969

Copyright © 1969

The Catholic University of America Press, Inc.

Library of Congress Card Catalogue Number: 68-31683
S.B.N.   8132-0253-1

CONTENTS

iii

PREFACE

To compile a bibilography of scholarship
on Gerard Manley Hopkins is not only to praise
the poet and his works but also to judge the
validity of his critics' efforts. Hopkins has
undoubtedly been underrated, overpraised, and
misinterpreted; but the variety of the entries
listed here attests to the widespread interest
in his poems and to the great appeal which they
have had. Although his poetry was neglected
and misunderstood during his lifetime and although his slim volume of poems was not first
published until almost thirty years after his
death, the generations of critics since 1918
have probably directed more attention to
Hopkins than to any other late-Victorian poet.
The number of critiques, articles, essays, and
books devoted to his contribution to English
letters is now well over a thousand.

*

This prefatory note stands, in part, as a
defense of a <u>chronological</u> bibliography.
Hopkins was a contemporary of Tennyson, Swin-
burne, and Matthew Arnold. Yet nothing about
his poetry has impressed his readers as being
"Victorian," neither his idiom, his imagery
and intensity, nor the "sprung rhythm" which
he claimed to have discovered. He considered
Victorian verse to be "Parnassian," embodying
"a language and style mastered...and at command
but employed without any fresh inspiration";[1]
and because of his connection with the modern
literary scene, only in the past few decades
has Hopkins come to be judged in relation
to his own time.

The criticism of Hopkins' poetry began
during his lifetime, among the small circle of
friends who constituted his audience. Though
the reactions expressed by Robert Bridges,
Richard Watson Dixon, and Coventry Patmore
exemplified most of the "decadent" late-
Victorian attitudes toward poetry, it is
significant that all three were poets dedicated
to their art and to the more technical problems
of craftsmanship. They had the advantage of
familiarity with Hopkins' theory of poetry and
his explanations and experiments. Yet all
three in varying degrees failed to recognize
the importance of his innovations.

The letters of Robert Bridges to Gerard
Manley Hopkins are not extant, but it is not
difficult to judge the tenor of the criticism
therein from the nature of Hopkins' response,
which seems always to be a plea for greater
tolerance and an indictment of an evaluation
based on prejudice. It was perhaps inevitable
that Bridges should apply to poetry a scale of
values which Hopkins could not share; the cause
lay, most certainly, in Bridges' deep instinc-
tive reaction against Hopkins' whole philosophy
of life--with its embodiment in his poetry.
Moreover, Bridges seems not to have understood
fully the rule-abiding nature of Hopkins'
sprung rhythm and the restrictions he placed
upon its freedom. Bridges censured the obscurity, and Hopkins pleaded with him to pay
attention to the most intelligible stanzas:

If you had done this you wd. have
liked it better and sent me some
serviceable criticisms, but now your
criticism is of no use, being only a
protest memorialising me against my
whole policy and proceedings.[2]

Richard Watson Dixon recognized immediately that Hopkins' poems possessed the char-
acteristics of genius, and his encouragement
was as constant as was his fear that Hopkins--
through devotion to his priesthood--might for-
sake poetry altogether. His reaction upon
first seeing the poems was an intuitive and
emotional expression of delight and astonish-
ment. But Dixon's was a deep and intense admiration, which has been regarded by some com-
mentators as exhibiting little more than a pre-
critical innocence; Claude Colleer Abbott, the
editor of Hopkins' letters, has called Dixon's
response approbation rather than criticism.

Coventry Patmore, the third friend to whom
Hopkins submitted his poems, was, unlike Bridges
and Dixon, an established poet. He also favored
experiment and innovation in prosody. Moreover, he was, like Hopkins, a convert to the
Catholic Church. These factors might lead one
to expect from him a sympathetic understanding
of Hopkins' intentions; but, if Hopkins cher-
ished any such expectation, then his hope was
disappointed.

Patmore did not fail to recognize Hopkins'
genius. But the strange rhythms and unprece-
dented alliteration and compounds of Hopkins'
verse seemed a denial of Patmore's own conception of poetry: he could not see how Hopkins'
creations could arise from "the spontaneous
expression of ... poetical feeling...."[3] His
was a Victorian as well as a personal standard--
and that is why he felt that the poems could
never have a popular appeal; that is why Patmore could not understand Bridges' and Dixon's
admiration.

Hopkins' contemporaries were of their
time, and rarely does custom permit the appre-
ciation of what is new. But if, to Bridges,

Hopkins' spiritually dedicated life was an
unfathomable mystery, then his poetry was
worth serious attention and criticism; and
Hopkins knew this. Aside from matters of taste,
many of Hopkins' poems had a great attraction
for Bridges and probably more often than is
recorded he expressed his approval and praise;
and no higher tribute could be given to any
poet than that recorded by Dixon: "Bridges
struck the truth long ago when he said to me
that your poems more carried him out of him-
self than those of anyone."[4] Dixon presumably
was unable to give the technical understanding
that came from Bridges, but he was in a better
position to appreciate Hopkins' lofty religious
ideals. He was greatly moved by the power and
strangeness of the verse, and, in a passage
which has become celebrated for its critical
penetration, Dixon isolated its unique quality:

> I can understand that your present
> position, seclusion and exercises
> would give to your writings a rare
> charm--something that I cannot de-
> scribe, but know to myself by the
> inadequate word terrible pathos--
> something of what you call temper
> in poetry: a right temper which
> goes to the point of the terrible;
> the terrible crystal.[5]

Patmore, although he faced the poetry with
almost complete misunderstanding, had a great
personal admiration for the man and priest whose
authority meant so much to him; he felt toward
Hopkins, as he later wrote to Bridges, "a rever-
ence and affection, the like of which I have
never felt for any other man...."[6] Thus Hopkins
did receive from his three friends something

which few men receive in abundance: admiration,
encouragement, and sincere criticism.
      W. H. Gardner, editor of the third and
fourth editions of Hopkins' Poems and author of
one of the most comprehensive works published
on Hopkins to date, in an attempt to avoid a
chronological survey of Hopkins' critical reception, has sought to group the early reviewers
and later critics according to their approxima-
tion to the attitudes of these three original
critics:

> . . . [R]eaders of Hopkins may be
> fairly divided into three main groups:
> first, the "school of Dixon" --those
> who, so to speak, swallow Hopkins
> whole (or very nearly) and relish the
> flavor; second, the "school of Bridges"
> --those who, accepting the style as
> authentic experiment but deploring the
> blemishes, follow the lead of the
> Editor by assiduously cultivating
> "tolerance" and searching for the rare
> beauties; third, the "school of
> Patmore" --those who feel the under-
> lying poetic power and even sense the
> beauties but reject the whole manner
> and style on a priori grounds.[7]

In varying degrees, most critics' attitudes
toward the poetry of Hopkins have tended to
parallel those of Dixon, Bridges, and Patmore.
This classification creates convenient divi-
sions and, especially when applied to the
years immediately following the first publica-
tion of Hopkins' Poems, valid ones. But it
does not supply a category for certain critics
who--like Gardner himself--in their unstinted

admiration for Hopkins might be identified
with the "school of Dixon," but whose critical
acumen relates them to Bridges. Furthermore,
this division does not provide for the class
of literary semanticists, the "new" critics
prominent since the 1930's, who have recognized
Hopkins' style--as authentic linguistic experi-
mentation--without any need of Bridges' "tolerance." Such a subtle grouping as Gardner has
presented does not serve to evaluate fully
Hopkins' contributions to English literature,
and it cannot present an accurate account of
the trends of Hopkins' critical reception.

In yet another grouping of Hopkins' critics,
Maurice Charney has attempted to catalog the
trends of the divided reactions of Bridges'
"Preface to Notes" in the 1918 Poems. (Spe-
cifically, the strictures of the Poet Laureate,
echoed so widely in the early reviews, were
three: "oddity" of style, "obscurity" of meaning, and a "naked encounter of sensualism and
asceticism" in the thought and imagery.) It
was Charney's purpose "to trace the development
of Hopkins criticism as an answer to these
three charges"; using Bridges' preface as a
schematized focal point for critical attitudes,
he considered the development of the later
criticism "as a defense of Hopkins against
Bridges."[8]

It is, of course, no exaggeration to say
that the "Preface to Notes" presents the out-
lines of Hopkins criticism since 1918; all the
scholarship since then has tended either to
accept Bridges' position, to qualify it, or
eventually completely to reverse it. But such
a grouping, like Charney's, necessarily imposes
confining limitations upon the student of
Hopkins criticism.

*

There is a good deal of truth in the sug-
gestion that a poet often has to create the
taste by which he is to be appreciated; and
herein lies another advantage of a chronological
bibliography of Hopkins criticism: such a
survey is almost a history of the transition
from Victorian to modern attitudes toward
poetry.

In recent years a major concern has arisen
in regard to the definitive placing of Hopkins
in the stream of English literature. Both the
Victorians and the "moderns" have claimed him,
and the claim of each has its merits. The
Victorians point out that of the four real
shapers of Hopkins' mind--Duns Scotus, Newman,
Ruskin, and Pater--three were his contemporaries; they maintain that his poems must be
considered in relation to late nineteenth-
century thought. The "moderns," on the other
hand, argue that Hopkins' work expresses the
same freedom of technique which has charac-
terized poetry since the 1920's, that his poems
are thus an integral part of contemporary literature. And so Hopkins continues to be a
controversial literary figure, and it remains
to be seen whether F. R. Leavis was correct
when he evaluated Hopkins' position in 1932:
"He is likely to prove, for our time and the
future, the only influential poet of the
Victorian age, and he seems to me the greatest."[9]

But the scholarship listed here has a
value beyond its application to Gerard Manley
Hopkins; for it mirrors in part the major
critical and literary trends of the past fifty
years:

Intensive analysis of individual
works of literature has more and more

> become the basis of criticism during
> the past twenty-five years.
> . . . .
> . . . modern explication probably
> begins with I. A. Richards. . . . In
> 1929 Richards published <u>Practical
> Criticism</u>, the result of having stu-
> dents write out comments on poems
> which he then analyzed and ultimately
> synthesized in lectures that attempted
> to find out what poetry does by examin-
> ing specific poems for what each did.
> Other books appeared at about the same
> time (as those by Empson and by Riding
> and Graves), for explication was in
> the air.[10]

It is significant to note that each work men-
tioned in this perceptive passage--Richards'
<u>Practical Criticism</u> (1929), William Empson's
<u>Seven Types of Ambiguity</u> (1930), and Laura
Riding and Robert Graves' <u>A Survey of Modernist
Poetry</u> (1928)--contributed a major statement not
only to English letters but also to Hopkins
criticism as well. The authors trained upon
Hopkins those methods of close examination of
the text and critical exegesis for which they
have become famous. They welcomed the difficulty;
indeed, in the obscurity of Hopkins' verse they
found a positive value, a "resistance" which
allowed for more complex responses in the
sensitive reader.

     It is not surprising, then, that Hopkins
became a test case in the struggle for the
recognition of modern poetry, which achieved a
certain intensity at Oxford and Cambridge
around 1930. W. B. Yeats argued that Hopkins'
style was merely "the last development of
poetic diction,"[11] that Hopkins was to be
counted among the decadents rather than the

innovators; his attitude was not unlike that
of Bridges, who had first challenged Hopkins'
poems with strictures on their "luxurious
experiments." But Richards, Empson, and F. R.
Leavis championed Hopkins as the classic ex-
ample of the modern poet. First published in
1918, Hopkins' Poems demanded attention from
readers and scholars who were also judging the
works of T. S. Eliot, E. E. Cummings, and a
host of other experimental writers; these works
demanded new modes of criticism, from which
Hopkins subsequently benefited.

    Thus the general trend from 1918 until
today has been toward the growing acceptance
of Hopkins; and even this is a valid index to
the chronological change which has taken place
in the scholarship through the years. Hopkins'
poetry has become a favorite critical objective
of the new attitudes toward "difficult" poetry
which were evolving fifty years ago: the
language of his poetry is so highly charged
that it seems to ask for analysis, and expli-
cators from the beginning have realized that
his verse repays study; the form of Hopkins'
extradordinary work has demanded notice not
merely because of its intrinsic interest but
also because it has illustrated the conflict
between freedom and discipline, between innovation and tradition, that is the essence of
what poetry is all about.

*

    The main objective in the compilation of
the present study has been consistency of purpose and treatment: the details are given in
the same order and form throughout--to facili-
tate complete and easy reference. Users of
bibliographies seldom give thought to the
breadth of the essentially communal and

cooperative task of every bibliographer. It
is impossible to name individually all those
whose assistance has made this work possible;
for librarians throughout the world have will-
ingly contributed their efforts. But a few
acknowledgements must be here recorded: the
library staff of The Catholic University of
America, Washington, D. C., and Woodstock
College and Theologiate, Woodstock, Maryland,
and The Library of Congress, for their help and
understanding; Sister Mary David, S.S.N.D.,
Reference Librarian, College of Notre Dame,
Baltimore, Maryland, for her kindness in allow-
ing me to use the Gerard Manley Hopkins Collec-
tion of Sister Roberta Melchner; Professors
Norton B. Crowell, Paul B. Davis, and Franklin
M. Dickey, Department of English, University
of New Mexico, for their wise judgment and
guidance; my family and friends, for their encouragement; and my wife, Donna, for her
criticism and patience.

Rollins College
Winter Park, Florida
March 17, 1969

NOTES

[1]The Correspondence of Gerard Manley Hopkins and Richard Watson Dixon, ed. Claude Colleer Abbott (London, 1955), p. 72.

[2]The Letters of Gerard Manley Hopkins to Robert Bridges, ed. Claude Colleer Abbott (London, 1955), pp. 46-47.

[3]Further Letters of Gerard Manley Hopkins including His Correspondence with Coventry Patmore, ed. Claude Colleer Abbott, 2nd ed., revised and enlarged (London, 1956), p. 355.

[4]The Correspondence of Gerard Manley Hopkins and Richard Watson Dixon, ed. Claude Colleer Abbott, 2nd (revised) impression (London, 1955), p. 100.

[5]Ibid., p. 80.

[6]Basil Champneys, Memoir and Correspondence of Coventry Patmore (London, 1900), II, p. 249.

[7]Gerard Manley Hopkins: A Study of Poetic Idiosyncrasy in Relation to Poetic Tradition (London, 1944), I, p. 211.

[8]"A Bibliographical Study of Hopkins Criticism: 1918-1949," Thought, XXV (June, 1950), 298.

[9]New Bearings in English Poetry (London, 1932), p. 193.

[10]George Arms, "A Note on Explication," The Western Review, XV (Autumn, 1950), 57-58.

[11]"Introduction," in The Oxford Book of Modern Verse 1892-1935 (New York, 1936), pp. xxxix-xl.

PART I

THE PUBLISHED WORKS OF
GERARD MANLEY HOPKINS

This is a list of editions and revisions
of editions of Hopkins' poems, letters, and
prose works. It also includes complete references to individual works first published
separately.

1863
1. "Winter with the Gulf Stream," Once A Week,
   VIII (February 14), 210.
   [First published poem; printed over
   "G. M. H."]

1865
2. "Barnfloor and Winepress," The Union Review,
   III, 579-580.
   [Printed over "G.M.H."]
3. Correspondence in The Church Times, III,
   No. 140 (October 7), unpaginated.
   [Signed: "G. H."]

1881
4. "Milton (translated from Dryden)," The
   Stonyhurst Magazine, I, No. 2 (July),
   35.
   [Hopkins' Latin version of Dryden's
   "Epigram on Milton"; published anony-
   mously.]

1882
5. Correspondence in Nature, XXVII (November
   16), 53.
   [Letter on natural phenomenon: "A
   Curious Halo."]

1

6.   "The Song of Chaucer's Clerk of Oxenford,
     'Angelus ad Virginem,'" The Month,
     XLIV, No. 211 (January), 100-111.
     [Modernization of Chaucer's hymn;
     published anonymously.]]

1883

7.   Correspondence in Nature, XXIX (November
     15), 55.
     [Letter on natural phenomenon: "Shadow-
     Beams in the East at Sunset."]
8.   "A Trio of Triolets," The Stonyhurst Maga-
     zine, I, No. 9 (March), 162.
     [Three comic triolets; published over
     Hopkins' pseudonym, "Bran."]

1884

9.   Correspondence in Nature, XXIX (January 3),
     222-223.
     [Letter on natural phenomenon: "The
     Remarkable Sunsets."]

1885

10. "Richard Watson Dixon," in A Manual of
     English Literature Historical and
     Critical, ed. Thomas Arnold, 5th ed.
     London: Longmans, Green & Co., pp.
     470-471.
     [Biographical and literary notice;
     contributed by Hopkins; published
     anonymously.]

1886

11. "Songs from Shakspeare, in Latin.   No. I.
     'Full fathom five they father lies,'"
     The Irish Monthly, XIV, No. 161 (November),
     628.
     [Hopkins' translation into Latin; pub-
     lished anonymously.]

1887

12. "First Fruits," in Bible Birthday Book,
     ed. Richard Watson Dixon. London:
     George Routledge & Sons, unpaginated
     (entry for May 25).
     [First stanza of "Morning Midday and
     Evening Sacrifice"; printed over
     "Hopkins."]

13. Letter on Spectral or Imagined Numbers,
     in: Manley Hopkins. The Cardinal
     Numbers. London: Sampson Low, Marston,
     Searle and Rivington, pp. 20-21.

14. "Songs from Shakspere in Latin. No. II.
     'Come unto these yellow sands,'" The
     Irish Monthly, XV, No. 164 (February),
     92.
     [Hopkins' translation into Latin;
     printed over "G. H."]

1888

15. Correspondence in The Stonyhurst Magazine,
     III (November), 236-237.
     [Letter on football; signed with a
     pseudonym: "Gymnosophist."]

16. The Royal Soceity. The Eruption of
     Krakatoa and Subsequent Phenomena.
     Report of the Krakatoa Committee of the
     Royal Society, ed. G. J. Symons, F.R.S.
     London: Trübner & Co., pp. viii, 172.
     [Selections from correspondence in
     Nature.]

1890

17. "Ad Mariam," Blandyke Papers, XXVI (May),
     130.

1893

18. "The Habit of Perfection," "To R. B.,"
     "Inversnaid," "The Candle Indoors,"
     "Spring," "The Starlight Night,"
     "Spring and Fall," and "A vision of the
     Mermaids," in The Poets and the Poetry
     of the XIXth Century, Vol. VIII: Robert
     Bridges and Contemporary Poets, ed.
     Alfred H. Miles. London: Hutchinson
     & Co., pp. 165-170.

1894

19. "Ad Mariam," The Stonyhurst Magazine, V,
     No. 72 (February), 233.
     [Hopkins' poem printed under a letter
     from a correspondent signed "O. S. J."]

1895

20. "The Elopement," The Oratory School Maga-
     zine, No. 13 (November), pp. 5-8.
     [Included in an anonymous essay, "Early
     Magazines"; this essay is the only re-
     cord of the verses which appear in a
     handwritten weekly journal, The Early
     Bird or The Tuesday Tomtit, edited by
     students and junior masters of the
     Oratory School, Edgbaston, in 1868.]

21. "Heaven Haven," "God's Grandeur," "Barn-
     floor and Winepress," "Morning Midday
     and Evening Sacrifice," and "(Thee
     God, I Come from . . .)," in Lyra
     Sacra: A Book of Religious Verse, ed.
     H[enry] C. Beeching. London: Methuen
     & Co., pp. 313-316.

22. "Mary Mother of Divine Grace Compared to
     the Air We Breathe," in A Book of
     Christmas Verse, ed. H[enry] C. Beech-
     ing. London: Methuen & Co., pp. 121-
     125.

1898
23. "Rosa Mystica," The Irish Monthly, XXVI,
    No. 299 (May), 234-235.
    [Reprinted in The Weekly Register
    (Westminster Diocese), May 7.]

1900
24. Nine letters from Hopkins to Coventry
    Patmore, in: Basil Champneys. Memoir
    and Correspondence of Coventry Patmore.
    London: George Bell & Sons, II,
    345-355.

1902
25. "Rosa Mystica" and "Mary Mother of Divine
    Grace Compared to the Air We Breathe,"
    in Carmina Mariana: An English An-
    thology of Verse in Honour of and in
    Relation to the Blessed Virgin Mary,
    ed. Orby Shipley, 2nd ed., 2nd ser.
    London: Burns and Oates, pp. 183-189.

1903
26. "Heaven-Haven," Living Age, 7th ser.,
    XVIII (January 10), 128.

1906
27. Extracts from Hopkins' "Journal," ed. J.
    G. MacLeod, S. J., in Letters and
    Notices, XXVIII, No. 163 (April),
    390-401.

1907
28. Extracts from Hopkins' "Journal," ed. J.
    G. MacLeod, S. J., in Letters and
    Notices, XXIX, No. 167 (April),
    129-135; No. 169 (October), 270-281.

1909
29. Letters from Hopkins to Dixon and Patmore,
     in: Rev. Joseph Keating. "Impressions
     of Father Gerard Hopkins, S. J.," The
     Month, CXIV, No. 542 (August), 152-
     153; No. 543 (September), 256-257.

1913
30. "The Starlight Night," in The Oxford Book
     of Victorian Verse, ed. Arthur Quiller-
     Couch. Oxford: Clarendon Press, p.
     691.

1915
31. "Nondum," The Month, CXXVI (September),
     246-247.

1916
32. "Spring and Fall," "In the Valley of the
     Elwy," "The Candle Indoors," "The
     Handsome Heart," "The Wreck of the
     Deutschland" [first stanza], and "The
     Habit of Perfection" [first two
     stanzas], in The Spirit of Man, ed.
     Robert Bridges. London: Longmans,
     Green & Co., unpaginated.

1917
33. "The Habit of Perfection," "God's Gran-
     deur," and "Mary Mother of Divine
     Grace Compared to the Air We Breathe,"
     in The Oxford Book of English Mystical
     Verse, ed. D. H. S. Nicholson and A.
     H. E. Lee. Oxford: Clarendon Press,
     pp. 353-359.
34. "The Starlight Night," "The Habit of
     Perfection," and "Spring," in Dreams
     and Images: An Anthology of Catholic
     Poets, ed. Joyce Kilmer. New York:
     Boni and Liveright, pp. 99-101.

1918

35. Poems of Gerard Manley Hopkins, now First Published, Edited with Notes by Robert Bridges, Poet Laureate. London: Humphrey Milford, Oxford University Press; 124 pp.

1919

36. "Rosa Mystica," The Month, CXXXIII, No. 659 (May), 339-340. [Omitted by Bridges in 1918 Poems.]

1920

37. "Dorothea and Theophilus," The Dublin Review, CLXVII, No. 334 (July-September), 45-43.
38. Extracts from Hopkins' "Journal," in The Dublin Review, CLXVII, No. 334 (July-September), 58-66.

1929

39. A Vision of the Mermaids. A Prize Poem dated Christmas, 1862 . . . and now for the first time printed in full. The poem is here published in a complete facsimile. London: Humphrey Milford, Oxford University Press; unpaginated.

1930

40. Poems of Gerard Manley Hopkins, Edited with notes by Robert Bridges. Second Edition With an Appendix of Additional Poems, and a Critical Introduction by Charles Williams. London: Oxford University Press; xvi, 159 pp.

1932

41. Letters from Hopkins to Bridges and Dixon,
     in: Robert Bridges. Three Friends:
     Memoirs of Digby Mackworth Dolben,
     Richard Watson Dixon, Henry Bradley.
     London: Oxford University Press, pp.
     103-104, 239-241, et passim.

1935

42. The Correspondence of Gerard Manley Hopkins
     and Richard Watson Dixon, Edited with
     notes & an Introduction by Claude
     Colleer Abbott. London: Oxford Uni-
     versity Press; xxxi, 192 pp.

43. Extracts from Hopkins' notebooks and early
     poems, including "A Soliloquy of one of
     the Spies left in the Wilderness," "New
     Readings," "Where Art Thou Friend,"
     "The Beginning of the End," "To Oxford,"
     and "See how Spring," in The Criterion,
     XV, No. 58 (October), 1-17.

44. The Letters of Gerard Manley Hopkins to
     Robert Bridges, Edited with notes &
     an Introduction by Claude Colleer
     Abbott. London: Oxford University
     Press; xlvii, 322 pp.

1936

45. "On a Piece of Music," text by Geoffrey
     Bliss, in The Month, CLXVII, No. 860
     (February), 160-167.
     [Discussion and final text of Hopkins'
     fragment.]

46. "The Woodlark," text by Geoffrey Bliss,
     in The Month, CLXVII, No. 864 (June),
     528-535.

     [Discussion and final text of Hopkins'
     fragment.]

47. Selections from Hopkins' sermons, in <u>The
     Tablet</u>, CLXVIII (November 14), 665-668;
     (November 21), 703-704; (November 28),
     739-740; (December 5), 772; (December
     12), 830-831; (December 19), 864-865.
     [The sermons, in order of appearance:
     "A Sermon on the Paraclete," "God's
     First Kingdom: Its Rise and Fall in
     Earthly Paradise," "(The Fall of Man),"
     "The Immaculate Conception," "(Our Lord
     Jesus Christ, my brethern, is our Hero),"
     "The Sacred Heart."]

                    1937
48. <u>The Note-Books and Papers of Gerard Manley
     Hopkins</u>, Edited with Notes and a Pre-
     face by Humphry House. London: Ox-
     ford University Press; xxxvi, 474 pp.
49. <u>Poems of Gerard Manley Hopkins</u>, Edited
     with notes by Robert Bridges. Second
     Edition With an Appendix of Additional
     Poems, and a Critical Introduction by
     Charles Williams, re-issued in "The
     Oxford Bookshelf." London: Oxford
     University Press; xvi, 159 pp.

                    1938
50. <u>Further Letters of Gerard Manley Hopkins
     including his Correspondence with
     Coventry Patmore</u>, Edited with Notes and
     an Introduction by Claude Coller Abbott.
     London: Oxford University Press,
     xxxviii, 297 pp.

                    1945
51. <u>Selections from the Note-Books of Gerard
     Manley Hopkins</u> (The Poets of the Year),
     ed. T[heodore] Weiss. Norfolk, Con-
     necticut: New Directions; unpaginated.

52.   Some Poems of Gerard Manley Hopkins.
      London: Michael White; 32 pp.

                    1947
53.   "Iesu, Dulcis Memoria," "Odi Profanum
      Vulgus," and "Persicos Odi," America,
      LXXVII, No. 23 (September 26), 633-635.
      [Three translations by Hopkins, here
      first published; reprinted in The
      Tablet, CXC (September 27), 199.]
54.   Extracts from Hopkins' "Journal," in
      Letters and Notices, LV, No. 295 (May),
      147-155; No. 296 (September), 223-235.
      [Includes selections for May 2-June 5,
      1866.]

                    1948
55.   Extracts from Hopkins' "Journal," in
      Letters and Notices, LVI, No. 297
      (January), 18-29; No. 298 (May), 100-
      104.
      [Includes selections for July 6-Sep-
      tember 8, 1866.]
56.   Letter from Hopkins to E. H. Coleridge,
      dated September 3, 1862, ed. J. M. G.
      Blakiston, in The Times Literary
      Supplement (London), September 25, p.
      548.
      [Includes three poems: "Il Mystico,"
      "A Windy Day in Summer," and "(A frag-
      ment of anything you like)."]
57.   Poems of Gerard Manley Hopkins, the First
      Edition with Preface and Notes by
      Robert Bridges.   Edited with additional
      Poems, Notes, and a Biographical Intro-
      duction by W. H. Gardner.   Third
      [English] Edition, First [American]
      Edition.   London & New York: Oxford
      University Press; xxvi, 292 pp.

58. Poems of Gerard Manley Hopkins. Mt.
     Vernon, New York: Peter Pauper Press,
     [no date] , unpaginated.

                    1950
59. Extracts from Hopkins' "Journal," in The
     Month, n. s., IV, No. 6 (December),
     375-384.
     [Reprinted from Letters and Notices,
     1947-1948.]
60. Glory Be to God for Dappled Things.
     Denver: Printed by Theodor Jung at
     his Cloverleaf Press; unpaginated.

                    1953
61. Correspondence in The Stonyhurst Magazine,
     XXI (April), 168-169.
     [Letter on football; signed with a
     pseudonym: "Gymnosophist"; reprinted
     from The Stonyhurst Magazine, III
     (November, 1888), 236-237.]
62. A Hopkins Reader. Selected and with an
     Introduction by John Pick. London &
     New York: Oxford University Press;
     xxvii, 317 pp.
63. Poems and Prose of Gerard Manley Hopkins,
     selected with an introduction and notes
     by W. H. Gardner. London: Penguin
     Books Ltd.; xxxvii, 252 pp.
64. Selected Poems of Gerard Manley Hopkins,
     Edited with an Introduction and Notes
     by James Reeves. London: William
     Heinemann; xxviii, 103 pp.

                    1954
65. Selected Poems of Gerard Manley Hopkins,
     ed. Francis Meynell. Limited edition.
     London: The Nonesuch Press; 104 pp.

1955

66. The Correspondence of Gerard Manley Hopkins
and Richard Watson Dixon, Edited with
notes and an Introduction by Claude
Colleer Abbott. Second Impression,
revised. London: Oxford University
Press; xxi, 192 pp.

67. "Gerard Manley Hopkins on Bridges," in
Robert Bridges: Poetry & Prose, ed.
John Sparrow. Oxford: Clarendon
Press, pp. xxi-xxiii.
[Selections from letters to Bridges.]

68. The Letters of Gerard Manley Hopkins to
Robert Bridges, Edited with notes & an
Introduction by Claude Colleer Abbott.
Second Impression, revised. London:
Oxford University Press; xlvii, 322 pp.

1956

69. Further Letters of Gerard Manley Hopkins
including his Correspondence with
Coventry Patmore, Edited with Notes
and an Introduction by Claude Colleer
Abbott. Second Edition, revised and
enlarged. London: Oxford University
Press; xliii, 465 pp.

70. Poems of Gerard Manley Hopkins, ed. W. H.
Gardner. Third edition, fifth impres-
sion, revised, with additional poems.
London & New York: Oxford University
Press; xxvi, 307 pp.

71. "St. Thecla," Studies, XLV, No. 178
(Summer), 187.
[Here first published; reprinted in
The Month, n. s., XVI, No. 1 (July),
12-13.]

1957

72. "Persephone," America, XCVII, No. 18
(August 3), 464-465.
[Here first published.]
73. Selected Poems of Gerard Manley Hopkins,
Edited with an Introduction and Notes
by James Reeves. New York: The
Macmillan Company; xxviii, 103 pp.

1958

74. Six new letters of Hopkins, ed. Graham
Storey, in The Month, n. s., XIX, No.
5 (May), 263-270.
[Letters from Hopkins to his father
(December 23, 1871, and July 5, 1884);
from Hopkins to Katherine Tynan
(November 14, 1886; June 2, 1887; July
8, 1887; September 15, 1888).]

1959

75. The Journals and Papers of Gerard Manley
Hopkins, Edited by Humphry House,
Completed by Graham Storey. London:
Oxford University Press; xxxiii, 579
pp.
76. The Sermons and Devotional Writings of
Gerard Manley Hopkins, edited by
Christopher Devlin, S.J., London:
Oxford University Press; xiv, 370 pp.

1966

77. A Hopkins Reader, selections from the
writings of Gerard Manley Hopkins,
edited with an introduction by John
Pick. Revised and enlarged edition.
Garden City, New York: Image Books;
439 pp.

1967

78. Hopkins, Selections Chosen and edited by
    Graham Storey (New Oxford English
    Series). London: Oxford University
    Press; vii, 206 pp.

79. The Poems of Gerard Manley Hopkins.
    Fourth Edition based on the First
    Edition of 1918 and enlarged to incor-
    porate all known Poems and Fragments.
    Edited with additional Notes, a Fore-
    word on the Revised Text, and a new
    Biographical and Critical Introduction
    by W. H. Gardner and N. H. MacKenzie.
    London & New York: Oxford University
    Press; lxvi, 362 pp.

PART II

CRITICISM OF THE WORKS OF
GERARD MANLEY HOPKINS

This is a list of studies of Hopkins' life
and works in books (and reviews of books) and
articles in journals and periodicals; it also
includes other significant references to the
poet which have appeared in passing or in
minor publications. Poems dedicated to Hopkins
are cited only when they reveal admiration of
or influence upon a major literary figure.

1873

1. Clarke, Marcus. "Holiday Peak or Mount-
    Might-Ha-Been," Holiday Peak and Other
    Tales. Melbourne, Australia: G.
    Robertson, pp. 8-10.
    [Story in which Hopkins is a character
    named "Gerard."]

1882

2. Tradleg, Nitram [E. Martin Geldart]. A
    Son of Belial: Autobiographical
    Sketches. London: Trübner & Co., pp.
    156, 168, et passim.
    [Story in which Hopkins is a character
    named "Gerontius Manley."]

1887

3. Dixon, Richard Watson. Lyrical Poems.
    Oxford: H. Daniel.
    ["Dedicated to the Reverend Gerard
    Hopkins, by the Author."]

1889

4.   Anon. "Gerard Manley Hopkins," The Free-
     man's Journal [Dublin], June 10, p. 5.
     [Notice of Hopkins' death.]

1890

5.   Anon. "Father Gerard Hopkins," Letters
     and Notices, XX, No. 99 (March), 173-
     179.
     [Notice of Hopkins' death.]

1892

6.   Boas, Frederic. "Gerard Manley Hopkins,"
     Modern English Biography. London:
     Truro, Netherton & Worth, I, 1534.

1893

7.   Bridges, Robert. "Gerard Hopkins. 1844-
     1889," in The Poets and the Poetry of
     the XIXth Century. Vol. VIII: Robert
     Bridges and Contemporary Poets, ed.
     Alfred H. Miles. London: Hutchinson
     & Co., pp. 161-164.

1894

8.   Bridges, Robert. Shorter Poems. Oxford:
     H. Daniel, II, 3.
     [Ode: "To the Memory of G. M. H."]

1900

9.   Champneys, Basil. Memoir and Correspond-
     ence of Coventry Patmore. London:
     George Bell & Sons, II, 345-355, et
     passim.

1902

10. Russell, Rev. Matthew, S.J. "Poets I Have
     Known. V: Katherine Tynan," Donahoe's
     Magazine, XLVII, No. 4 (April), 389-406.

1905

11. Gosse, Edmund. Coventry Patmore. London:
     Hodder & Stoughton, p. 169.

1909

12. Brégy, Katherine. "Gerard Hopkins. An
     Epitaph and an Appreciation," The
     Catholic World, LXXXVIII, No. 526
     (January), 433-447.
13. Keating, Rev. Joseph. "Impressions of
     Father Gerard Hopkins, S.J.," The Month,
     CXIV, No. 541 (July), 59-68; No. 542
     (August), 151-160; No. 543 (September),
     246-258.

1910

14. Brégy, Katherine. "Coventry Patmore,"
     The Catholic World, XC, No. 540 (March),
     803.
15. Saintsbury, George. A History of English
     Prosody. London: Macmillan and Co.,
     Ltd., III, 391.

1912

16. Brégy, Katherine. The Poet's Chantry.
     London: Herbert & Daniel, pp. 70-88.
     [Reprinted from The Catholic World,
     January, 1909.]
17. Lechmere, W. L. "Oxford: 1863-1867."
     The Oxford and Cambridge Review, No. 19
     (May), pp. 73-113.

1913

18. K[eating], J[oseph]. "The Poetry of Father
     Gerard Hopkins, S.J.," The Month, CXXI,
     No. 588 (June), 643-644.
19. Warren, T[homas] Herbert. Robert Bridges,
     Poet Laureate: Readings from Poems.
     Oxford: Clarendon Press, p. 16.

1914

20. Kilmer, Joyce. "The Poetry of Gerard
     Hopkins," Poetry, IV, No. 6 (September),
     241-245.

1916

21. Kilmer, Joyce. "Father Gerard Hopkins,
     S.J.," Studies, V, No. 17 (March), 106.
     [Poem.]
22. MacDonagh, Thomas. Literature in Ireland:
     Studies Irish and Anglo-Irish. London:
     T. Fisher Unwin, p. 229.
23. Neenan, Sister Mary Pius. Some Evidences
     of Mysticism in English Poetry of the
     Nineteenth Century. Unpublished M.A.
     thesis, The Catholic University of
     America, p. 76.
24. Saintsbury, George. The Nineteenth Cen-
     tury, II, in The Cambridge History of
     English Literature, ed. A. W. Ward
     and A. R. Waller. London: Cambridge
     University Press, XIII, 234, n. 1.

1917

25. Caine, Hall. Correspondence in The New
     Statesman, IX (June 23), 277.
     [Reply to Hone, in The New Statesman,
     June 9.]
26. Dubliner. Correspondence in The New
     Statesman, IX (June 23), 277.
     [Reply to Hone, in The New Statesman,
     June 9.]
27. Hone, J. M. "Gerard Hopkins," The New
     Statesman, IX (June 9), 231-232.

1918

28. Bridges, Robert. "Preface to Notes," in
     Poems of Gerard Manley Hopkins, now
     First Published. London: Oxford
     University Press, pp. 94-101.

29. Hogan, Aloysius J., S.J. "Father Hopkins'
    Poetry," America, XVIII, No. 19
    (February 16), 477-478.
30. Kilmer, Joyce. "Father Gerard Hopkins,
    S.J.," in Joyce Kilmer: Memoir and
    Poems, ed. Robert C. Holliday. New
    York: George Doran, p. 138.
    [Poem; reprinted from Studies, March,
    1916.]

                    1919
31. B., C. "Reminiscences of Father Gerard
    Hopkins," The Month, CXXXIV, No. 662
    (August), 158-159.
[28]. Bridges, Robert. Poems of Gerard Manley
    Hopkins. 1918.
    32. Anon. in The Catholic Book Club Notes,
        XXIII, No. 246 (April), 52-53.
    33. Anon. in The Dial, LXVI, No. 791 (May 31),
        572.
    34. Anon. in The Methodist Recorder [London],
        May 29, p. 9.
    35. Anon. in The Oxford Magazine, XXXVII (May
        23), 310-311.
    36. Anon. in Saturday Westminster Gazette,
        LIII (March 8), 13-14.
    37. Anon. in The Tablet, CXXXIII (April 5),
        420-422.
    38. Anon. in The Universe [London], March 14,
        p. 2.
    39. [Bain, Robert (?)]. in The Glasgow Herald,
        January 2, p. 3.
    40. [Clutton-Brock, Arthur]. in The Times
        Literary Supplement (London), January
        9, p. 19.
    41. Guiney, Louise Imogen. in The Ave Maria,
        n. s., IX, No. 14 (April 5), 433-435.
    42. Guiney, L[ouise] I. in The Month, CXXXIII,
        No. 657 (March), 205-214.

43. Guiney, Louise Imogen. in The Universe
    [London], March 21, p. 10.
    [Reply to The Universe, March 14, and
    Saturday Westminster Gazette, March 8.]
44. Henry, Michael. in Everyman, XIII
    (February 8), 416-417.
45. Lappin, Henry A. in The Catholic World,
    CIX, No. 652 (July), 501-512.
46. Maynard, Theodore. in America, XX, No.
    21 (March 1), 533-534.
47. Maynard, Theodore. in The New Witness,
    XIII, No. 325 (January 24), 259-260.
48. McBrien, Peter. in The Irish Rosary
    Literary Supplement [Dublin], XXIII
    (June), 473-478.
49. [Moore, F. C.]. in The Spectator, CXXII
    (May 10), 599.
50. M[urry], J. M[iddleton]. in The Athenaeum,
    No. 4649 (June 6), pp. 425-426.
51. O'Neill, G[eorge, S.J.]. in Studies,
    VIII, No. 30 (June), 331-335.
52. [Russell, Rev. Matthew, S.J.]. in The
    Irish Monthly, XLVII, No. 554 (August),
    441-448.
53. [Shanks, Edward]. in The New Statesman,
    XII, No. 310 (March 15), 530.
54. Harting, E. M. "Gerard Hopkins and Digby
    Dolben," The Month, CXXXIII, No. 658
    (April), 285-289.
55. O'Neill, George, S.J. "Gerard Hopkins,"
    Essays on Poetry. Dublin: The Talbot
    Press Ltd., pp. 117-138.

1920
[28] . Bridges, Robert. Poems of Gerard Manley
    Hopkins. 1918.
56. Page, Frederick. in The Dublin Review,
    CLXVII, No. 334 (July-September), 40-45.

57. Feeney, Leonard, S. J. "Father Hopkins'
    Mystic Songs," America, XXIII, No. 2
    (May 1), 41.
    [Poem.]
58. Murry, J. Middleton. "Gerard Manley
    Hopkins," Aspects of Literature. Lon-
    don: W. Collins Sons & Co. Ltd., pp.
    52-61.
59. Plures. "Father Gerard Hopkins. His
    Character," The Dublin Review, CLXVII,
    No. 334 (July-September), 47-58.
60. Underhill, Evelyn. The Essentials of
    Mysticism and Other Essays. London:
    J. M. Dent & Sons Ltd., pp. 71-72.

                    1921
[28]. Bridges, Robert. Poems of Gerard Manley
    Hopkins. 1918.
    61. Sapir, Edward. in Poetry, XVIII, No. 6
        (September), 330-336.
62. Kilmer, Joyce. "The Poetry of Gerard
    Hopkins," in The Circus and Other
    Essays and Fugitive Pieces by Joyce
    Kilmer, ed. Robert Cortes Holliday.
    New York: George H. Doran Company,
    pp. 180-185.
    [Reprinted from Poetry, September, 1914.]
63. Omond, T. S. English Metrists: Being A
    Sketch of English Prosodical Criticism
    from Elizabethan Times to the Present
    Day. Oxford: Clarendon Press, p. 263.

                    1922
64. Shuster, George N. The Catholic Spirit
    in Modern English Literature. New
    York: The Macmillan Company, pp. 115-
    121.

1923

[28]. Bridges, Robert. Poems of Gerard Manley
       Hopkins. 1918.
    65. Maynard, Theodore. in The Freeman, VIII,
        No. 189 (October 24), 156-157.
        [Condensed from America, March 1, 1919.]
66. Monroe, Harriet, and Alice Corbin Hender-
    son. The New Poetry: An Anthology of
    Twentieth-Century Verse in English.
    New and enlarged edition. New York:
    The Macmillan Company, pp. xlv-xlviii.
67. Porter, Alan. "Difficult Beauty," The
    Spectator, CXXX (January 13), 66.

1924

[28]. Bridges, Robert. Poems of Gerard Manley
       Hopkins. 1918.
    68. Putnam, Sam. in Chicago Evening Post,
        May 30, p. 7.

1925

69. Crowley, Austin. "Gerard Hopkins," The
    Boston College Stylus, XXXVIII, No. 4
    (January), 239-241.
70. Leslie, Shane. An Anthology of Catholic
    Poets. London: Burns Oates & Wash-
    bourne Ltd., pp. 12-15.

1926

71. Fry, Roger, and E. A. Lowe. "English
    Handwriting with Thirty-four Facsimile
    Plates and Artistic & Paleographical
    Criticisms," S. P. E.[Society of Pure
    English] Tract No. XXIII, plate 33,
    pp. 90-91.
72. Richards, I. A. "Gerard Hopkins," The
    Dial, LXXXI (September), 195-203.

1927
73. Richards. I. A. "Gerard Hopkins," The
    Cambridge Review, XLIX (October 28),
    49-51.
74. Robinson, Henry Morton. "Gerard Manley
    Hopkins: A Preface," The Commonweal,
    VII, No. 8 (December 28), 869-871.
75. Walsh, Thomas, ed. The Catholic Anthology.
    New York: The Macmillan Company, pp.
    534-535.

1928
76. Brown, Alec. "Gerard Hopkins and Asso-
    ciative Form," The Dublin Magazine,
    n. s., III, No. 2 (April-June), 6-20.
77. Lahey, Gerald F., S.J. "Gerard Manley
    Hopkins," America, XXXIX, No. 26
    (October 6), 619-620.
78. Riding, Laura, and Robert Graves. A
    Survey of Modernist Poetry. New York:
    Doubleday, Doran & Company, Inc., pp.
    90-94.

1929
79. N[orth], J[essica] N. "Quality in Mad-
    ness," Poetry, XXXIV, No. 5 (August),
    270-273.
80. Richards, I. A. Practical Criticism: A
    Study of Literary Judgment. London:
    Kegan Paul, Trench, Trübner & Co.
    Ltd., pp. 80-90.

1930
81. Barrett, Alfred, S.J. "As the Air We
    Breathe," The Ave Maria, n. s., XXXI,
    No. 10 (March 8), 289-291.
82. Burke, Molly M. "Gerard Manley Hopkins,"
    The Commonweal, XII, No. 19 (September
    10), 459-460.

83. Empson, William. Seven Types of Ambiguity.
London: Chatto & Windus, pp. 284-286.

84. Fathers of The Society of Jesus, eds. A
Page of Irish History: Story of Uni-
versity College, Dublin 1883-1909.
Dublin and Cork: The Talbot Press
Limited, pp. 105-106, et passim.

85. Lahey, G[erald] F., S.J. Gerard Manley
Hopkins. London: Oxford University
Press; 172 pp.

86. Anon. in The Canadian Forum [Toronto],
XI, No. 121 (October), 22-23.

87. Anon. in The New York Times Book Review,
July 27, p. 12.

88. Anon. in The Times Literary Supplement
(London), July 17, p. 593.

89. Anon. in The Times Literary Supplement
(London), December 25, p. 1099.

90. Binsse, H. L. in The Saturday Review of
Literature, VII, No. 3 (August 9),33-
34.

91. Dilly Tante [Stanley Kunitz] . in Wilson
Bulletin, V, No. 1 (September), 61.

92. Dilly Tante [Stanley Kunitz] . in Wilson
Bulletin, V, No. 4 (December) 256-258.

93. G., R. in America, XLIII, No. 25
(September 27), 600.

94. O., E. in The Tablet (Literary Supplement),
December 6, pp. 767-768.

95. O'Brien, Justin. in The Bookman, LXXI,
No. 4 (July), 447.

96. Pickman, Hester. in The Hound & Horn, IV,
No. 1 (October-December), 118-127.

97. Schneider, Isidor. in The Nation, CXXX
(April 16), 456-458.

98. Sykes, Gerald. in New York Evening Post,
August 9, pp. 5-6.

99. Underhill, Evelyn. in The Spectator, CXLV
(September 6), 318.

100. Lahey, G. F. "Hopkins and Newman," The
      Commonweal, XII, No. 8 (June 25), 211-
      213.
101. [Leahy, Maurice] . "The Late Poet Laure-
      ate and Father Gerard Hopkins,"
      Carmina, No. 2 (September), p. 22.
102. Moore, T. Sturge. "Style or Beauty in
      Literature," The Criterion, IX, No.
      37 (July), 591-603.
103. Moran, Eugene A. Correspondence in The
      Commonweal, XII, No. 23 (October 8),
      582.
      [Reply to M. M. Burke, in The Common-
      weal, September 10.]
104. Williams, Charles. "Introduction to the
      Second Edition," Poems of Gerard
      Manley Hopkins . . . Second Edition.
      London: Oxford University Press, pp.
      ix-xvi.
      105. Anon. in The Commonweal, XIII, No. 2
            (November 12), 32-33.
      [88]. Anon. in The Times Literary Supplement
            (London) July 17, p. 593.
      [89]. Anon. in The Times Literary Supplement
            (London), December 25, p. 1099.
      [90]. Binsse, H. L. in The Saturday Review of
            Literature, VII, No. 3 (August 9), 33-
            34.
      [92]. Dilly Tante [Stanley Kunitz] . in Wilson
            Bulletin, V, No. 4 (December), 256-
            258.
      [94]. O., E. in The Tablet (Literary Supple-
            ment), December 6, pp. 767-768.
      [96]. Pickman, Hester. in The Hound & Horn,
            IV, No. 1 (October-December), 118-127.
106. Zabel, M. D. "Gerard Manley Hopkins:
      Poetry as Experiment and Unity,"
      Poetry, XXXVII, No. 3 (December), 152-
      161.

1931
107.   Coblentz, Catherine Cate.   "A Catholic
       Poet Comes into His Own," The Ave
       Maria, n. s., XXXIII, No. 6 (February
       7), 161-163.
108.   Grisewood, Harman.   "Gerard Manley Hopkins,
       S.J.," The Dublin Review, CLXXXIX, No.
       379 (October), 213-226.
109.   Hope, Felix.   "Gerard Manley Hopkins,"
       The Irish Ecclesiastical Record, 5th
       ser., XXXVII, No. 6 (June), 561-570.
[85]. Lahey, G. F.   Gerard Manley Hopkins, 1930.
       110.   Cowley, Malcolm.   in New York Herald
              Tribune Books, March 8, pp. 1, 6.
       111.   Flanner, Hildegarde.   in The New Republic,
              LXV, No. 844 (February 4), 331-332.
       112.   M[eagher], M[argaret] C.   in The Catholic
              World, CXXXII, No. 792 (March), 754-
              756.
       113.   Read, Herbert.   in The Criterion, X, No.
              40 (April), 552-559.
       114.   Schappes, Morris U.   in The Symposium,
              II, No. 1 (January), 129-136.
115.   Lahey, Gerald F., S.J.   The Prosody of
       Gerard Manley Hopkins and Robert
       Bridges.   Unpublished M.A. thesis,
       Fordham University.
116.   Pryce-Jones, Alan.   "Gerard Manley
       Hopkins," The London Mercury, XXIV,
       No. 139 (May), 45-52.
117.   Williams, Charles.   Correspondence in
       The Times Literary Supplement (Lon-
       don), January 1, p. 12.
[104]. Williams, Charles.   Poems of Gerard
       Manley Hopkins.   1930.
       118.   Anon.   in The Booklist, XXVII, No. 7
              (March),   322.
       119.   Anon.   in The Nation, CXXXII, (January
              28), 105.

[110]. Cowley, Malcolm. in New York Herald
       Tribune Books, March 8, pp. 1, 6.
120. Deutsch, Babette. in New York Evening
       Post, March 14, p. 7.
[111]. Flanner, Hildegarde. in The New Re-
       public, LXV, No. 844 (February 4),
       331-332.
121. Grigson, Geoffrey. in The Saturday Re-
       view [London], CLI (February 14),
       237-238.
122. K., R. W. in Liverpool Post and Mercury,
       January 7, p. 4.
123. L[ittle], A[rthur]. in Studies, XX, No.
       77 (March), 165-167.
[112]. M[eagher], M[argaret] C. in The Catholic
       World, CXXXII, No. 792 (March), 754-
       756.
124. O'Brien, Justin. in The Bookman, LXXIII,
       No. 2 (April), 206-208.
[113]. Read, Herbert. in The Criterion, X,
       No. 40 (April), 552-559.
125. Routh, H. V. in The Year's Work in
       English Studies, XII, 286-287.
[114]. Schappes, Morris U. in The Symposium,
       II, No. 1 (January), 129-130.
126. Turner, W. J. in The Nineteenth Century
       and After, CIX, No. 648 (February),
       243-252.

                  1932
127. Boner, Harold A. Gerard Manley Hopkins.
       Unpublished M.A. thesis, Columbia
       University.
128. Burke, Francis, S.J. "The Muse Called
       Grace," Measure, I, No. 1 (Christmas),
       27-31.
       [Measure is the journal of the Gerard
       Manley Hopkins Poetry Society, George-
       town University, Washington, D. C.]

129. Caster, Sister Mary Cassilda, S.S.N.D.
      Elements of Mysticism in Hopkins.
      Unpublished M.A. thesis, DePaul Uni-
      versity.
130. D'Arcy, Martin C., S.J.   "Gerard Manley
      Hopkins, S.J.," Archivum Historicum
      Societatis Jesu [Rome], I, 118-122.
131. Haugh, Irene. "Gerald [sic] Manley
      Hopkins," The Irish Monthly, LX, No.
      706 (April), 220-227.
132. Kent, Muriel. "Gerard Manley Hopkins:
      Poet and Prosodist," The Bookman,
      LXXXI, No. 486 (March), 312-313.
133. Leavis, F. R. New Bearings in English
      Poetry: A Study of the Contemporary
      Situation. London: Chatto & Windus
      Ltd., pp. 159-193, et passim.
134. Olivero, Federico. Correnti Mistiche
      della Letteratura Inglese Moderna.
      Turin: Bocca, pp. 73-100.
135. Speranza, Ireneo [Don Giuseppe De Luca].
      in Il Frontespizio [Rome], VII, No. 7
      (July), 6.
136. Read, Herbert. Form in Modern Poetry.
      London: Sheed & Ward, pp. 44-54.
[104]. Williams, Charles. Poems of Gerard
      Manley Hopkins. 1930.
137. Koszul, A. in Revue Anglo-Américaine,
      IX (June), 451-452.
138. Stonier, G. W. in The New Statesman and
      Nation, n. s., III, No. 70 (June 25),
      836-838.

                      1933
139. Drew, Elizabeth. Discovering Poetry.
      New York: W. W. Norton & Company,
      Inc., pp. 82-85, et passim.
140. Elton, Oliver. The English Muse: A
      Sketch. London: G. Bell & Sons Ltd.,
      pp. 399-400.

141. Evans, B[enjamin] Ifor. English Poetry
     in the Later Nineteenth Century.
     London: Methuen & Co., Ltd., pp. 210-
     218, et passim.
142. Frazier, Alexander. The Prosody of
     Gerard Manley Hopkins. Unpublished
     M.A. thesis, University of Arizona.
143. House, Humphry. Correspondence in The
     Times Literary Supplement (London),
     March 2, p. 147.
     [Reply to Tierney, in TLS, February
     16.]
144. Kelly, Bernard. "The Joy of Chastity in
     the Poetry of Gerard Manley Hopkins,"
     Blackfriars, XIV, No. 163 (October),
     833-836.
145. Lahey, Gerald F. "Gerard Manley Hopkins,"
     The Commonweal, XVIII, No. 25 (October
     20), 581-584.
146. Mégroz, R[udolphe] L[ouis]. Modern
     English Poetry: 1882-1932. London:
     Ivor Nicholson & Watson, Ltd., pp. 61-
     63, 233-244, et passim.
147. Phare, Elsie Elizabeth (Mrs. Austin
     Duncan-Jones). The Poetry of Gerard
     Manley Hopkins: A Survey and Commen-
     tary. Cambridge: Cambridge Univer-
     sity Press; 149 pp.
   148. Anon. in Notes and Queries, CLXV, No.
        21 (November 25), 378.
   149. Browne, Wynyard. in The Bookman, LXXXV,
        No. 507 (December), 228-229.
   150. Clarke, Austin. in The Observer [London],
        November 26, p. 9.
   151. Plomer, William. in The Spectator, CLI
        (November 17), 712.
152. Phillipson, Dom Wulstan. "Gerard Manley
     Hopkins," The Downside Review, LI, No.
     146 (April), 326-348.

153. Read, Herbert. "Poetry and Belief in
          Gerard Manley Hopkins," New Verse,
          No. 1 (January), pp. 11-15.
154. Read, Herbert. "The Poetry of Gerard
          Manley Hopkins," in English Critical
          Essays: Twentieth Century, ed.
          Phyllis M. Jones. London: Oxford
          University Press, pp. 351-374.
155. Scott, Michael M., S.J. "Gerard Manley
          Hopkins," The Irish Monthly, LXI, No.
          725 (November), 715-720; No. 726
          (December), 786-792.
156. Stanier, R. S. Correspondence in The
          Times Literary Supplement (London),
          February 23, p. 127.
          [Reply to Tierney, in TLS, February
          16.]
157. Stonier, G. W. "Gerard Manley Hopkins,"
          Gog Magog and Other Critical Essays.
          London: J. M. Dent & Sons Ltd., pp.
          43-63.
158. Tierney, Michael. Correspondence in The
          Times Literary Supplement (London),
          February 16, p. 108.
          [Reply to Anon. review, in TLS,
          February 9.]
159. Tierney, Michael. Correspondence in The
          Times Literary Supplement (London),
          March 9, p. 167.
          [Reply to House, in TLS, March 2.]

                        1934
160. Bateson, F. W. English Poetry and the
          English Language: An Experiment in
          Literary History. Oxford: Clarendon
          Press, pp. 118-120.
161. Bremond, André. "La Poésie Naïve et
          Savante de Gérard Hopkins," Etudes,
          CCXXI, No. 1 (October 5), 23-49.

162. Brockington, A. Allen. Mysticism and
     Poetry: On a Basis of Experience.
     London: Chapman & Hall, Ltd., pp. 101-
     107, et passim.
163. Bullough, Goeffrey. The Trend of Modern
     Poetry. London: Oliver and Boyd, pp.
     22-25, et passim.
164. Day Lewis, C. A Hope for Poetry. Ox-
     ford: Basil Blackwell, pp. 6-13, 63-
     64, et passim.
165. Eliot, T. S. After Strange Gods: A
     Primer of Modern Heresy. New York:
     Harcourt, Brace and Company, pp. 51-53.
166. McGuire, D. P. The Poetry of Gerard
     Manley Hopkins. (English Association--
     Adelaide Branch, Pamphlet No. 2.)
     Adelaide, Australia: F. W. Preece &
     Sons; 31 pp.
[134]. Olivero, Federico. Correnti Mistiche
     della Letteratura Inglese Moderna.
     1932.
     167. De Luca, Giuseppe. in Nuova Antologia,
          7th ser., XII (April 16), 635-638.
     168. Gualtieri, F. M. in L'Italia Letteraria,
          X, No. 12 (March 25), 7.
[147]. Phare, Elsie Elizabeth. The Poetry of
     Gerard Manley Hopkins: A Survey and
     Commentary. 1933.
     169. Anon. in Letters and Notices, XLIX, No.
          272 (April), 89.
     170. Anon. in The Month, CLXIII, No. 835
          (January), 93.
     171. Anon. in The Nation, CXXXVIII (January
          24), 109.
     172. Anon. in The Times Literary Supplement
          (London), January 25, p. 57.
     173. Auden, W. H. in The Criterion, XIII,
          No. 52 (April), 497-500.

174. Benét, William Rose. in The Saturday
     Review of Literature, X, No. 32
     (February 24), 508.
175. Cock, Albert A. in Wessex, III, No. 1
     (June 1), 95-97.
[167]. De Luca, Giuseppe. in Nuova Antologia,
     7th ser., XII (April 16), 635-638.
176. Deutsch, Babette. in New York Herald
     Tribune Books, January 28, p. 2.
177. Downey, Harris. in The Commonweal, XIX,
     No. 24 (April 13), 667-668.
178. Fairley, Barker. in The Canadian Forum_
     [Toronto], XIV, No. 161 (February),
     186-187.
179. M[eagher], M[argaret] C. in The Catholic
     World, CXXXIX, No. 832 (July), 499.
180. R., M. R. in The Oxford Magazine, LII,
     No. 20 (May 17), 714.
181. R[oberts], M[ichael]. in The Adelphi,
     VIII, No. 1 (April), 76-77.
182. Stonier, G. W. in The Fortnightly Re-
     view, n. s., CXXXV, No. 807 (March),
     374.
183. T[ierney], M[ichael]. in Studies, XXIII,
     No. 89 (March), 80.
184. Walton, Eda Lou. in The New York Times
     Book Review, January 28, p. 2.
185. Wolff, Lucien. in Revue Anglo-Américaine,
     XI (August), 546-547.
186. Sitwell, Edith. Aspects of Modern Poetry.
     London: Gerald Duckworth and Company,
     pp. 51-72.
187. Slattery, James J. "Some Bibliographical
     References on Gerard Manley Hopkins,
     S.J.: 1845 [sic] - 1889," The
     Catholic Library World, V, No. 5,
     (January 15), 36.

188. Surtz, Edward L., S.J. Religious Aspect
      of the Poetry of Gerard Manley Hopkins.
      Unpublished M.A. thesis, Xavier Uni-
      versity.

                    1935
189. Abbott, C. Colleer. Correspondence in
      The Times Literary Supplement (Lon-
      don), March 21, p. 176.
190. Abbott, Claude Colleer. "Introduction,"
      The Correspondence of Gerard Manley
      Hopkins and Richard Watson Dixon.
      London: Oxford University Press, pp.
      xiii-xxxi.
                    [and]
191. Abbott, Claude Colleer. "Introduction,"
      The Letters of Gerard Manley Hopkins
      to Robert Bridges. London: Oxford
      University Press, pp. xv-xlvii.
      192. Anon. in Letters and Notices, L, No. 277
            (July), 169-170.
      193. Anon. in Life and Letters, XI, No. 62
            (February), 613-615.
      194. Anon. in The Springfield Republican
            [Massachusetts], February 24, p. 7.
      195. Anon. in The Times Literary Supplement
            (London), January 31, p. 59.
      196. Burdette, Osbert. in The Nineteenth
            Century and After, CXVII, No. 696
            (February), 234-241.
      197. Chew, Samuel C. in The Yale Review, XXV,
            No. 1. (September), 209-212.
      198. Day Lewis, C. in The New Republic,
            LXXXIII (May 22), 52.
      199. De Selincourt, Basil. in The Observer
            [London], January 20, p. 5.
      200. Deutsch, Babette. in New York Herald
            Tribune Books, March 17, pp. 1-2.

201. Dobrée, Bonamy. in The Spectator, CLIV (January 11), 53.
202. Downey, Harris. in The Virginia Quarterly Review, XI, No. 3 (July), 458-461.
203. Keating, Joseph. in The Month, CLXV, No. 848 (February), 125-136.
204. [Kunitz, Stanley]. in Wilson Bulletin, IX, No. 9 (May), 491-492.
205. Larsson, Raymond. in The Commonweal, XXII, No. 8 (June 21), 219-221.
206. Leavis, F. R. in Scrutiny, IV, No. 2 (September), 216-231.
207. Leslie, Shane. in The Ave Maria, n. s., XLI, No. 15 (April 13), 456-458.
208. Leslie, Shane. in The Saturday Review of Literature, XI, No. 35 (March 16), 549-550.
209. Lynam, Thomas J. in America, LII, No. 24 (March 23), 574.
210. Marsden, M. in Music and Letters, XVI, No. 2 (April), 158-159.
211. M[eagher], M[argaret] C. in The Catholic World, CXLII, No. 847 (October), 119-120.
212. Morrison, Theodore. in The Atlantic Monthly, CLVI, No. 3 (September), 6-8.
213. Phillipson, Dom Wulstan. in The Downside Review, LIII, No. 154 (April), 210-228.
214. Read, Herbert. in The Criterion, XIV, No. 56 (April), 478-482.
215. Roberts, Michael. in The London Mercury, XXXI, No. 185 (March), 480-481.
216. Routh, H. V. in The Year's Work in English Studies, XVI, 331-332.
217. Shewring, W. H. in Blackfriars, XVI, No. 181 (April), 265-271.
218. Stonier, G. W. in The New Statesman and Nation, n. s., IX, No. 205 (January 26), 108.

219. Walker, M. E. in The New York Times
     Book Review, March 10, p. 2.
220. Walton, Eda Lou. in The Nation, CXLI,
     (July 24), 109-111.
221. Warren, C. Henry. in The Fortnightly,
     n. s., CXXXVII (April), 503-504.
222. Alexander, Calvert, S.J. The Catholic
     Literary Revival: Three Phases in
     its Development from 1845 to the
     Present. Milwaukee, Wisconsin: The
     Bruce Publishing Company, pp. 71-85.
223. Behn, Irene. "Gerard Manley Hopkins
     und Seine Dichtung," Hochland [Munich],
     XXXII, No. 8 (May), 148-169.
224. Crehan, J. H. "Poetry and Religious
     Life: The Case of Gerard Manley
     Hopkins, S.J.," The Month, CLXVI,
     No. 858 (December), 493-503.
225. Deutsch, Babette. This Modern Poetry.
     New York: W. W. Norton & Co., Inc.,
     pp. 173-185, et passim.
226. Devlin, Christopher, S.J. "The Ignatian
     Inspiration of Gerard Hopkins," Black-
     friars, XVI, No. 189 (December), 887-
     900.
227. Downey, Harris. "A Poem Not Understood,"
     The Virginia Quarterly Review, XI,
     No. 4 (October), 506-517.
228. Emerson, Dorothy. "Gerard Manley Hopkins,"
     Scholastic, XXVI, No. 16 (May 25), 10.
229. Fairley, Barker. "Charles Doughty and
     Modern Poetry," The London Mercury,
     XXXII, No. 188 (June), 128-137.
230. Gallagher, Donald A. "The Originality
     of Gerard Manley Hopkins," The Fleur
     De Lis, XXXIV, No. 2 (March), 34-44.

231. Hopkins, L. C. Correspondence in The
        Times Literary Supplement (London),
        March 14, p. 160.
        [Reply to Plowman, in TLS, February
        28, affirming Hopkins' birthdate as
        July 28, 1844.]
232. James, Stanley B. "The Sacrifice of
        Song," The Catholic World, CXLI (June),
        290-295.
233. Junkersfeld, Sister M. Julienne, S.S.N.D.
        History and the Critical Reception of
        the Poems of Gerard Manley Hopkins, S.
        J. Unpublished M.A. thesis, Loyola
        University [Chicago].
234. K[eating], J[oseph]. "Fr. Gerard Hopkins
        and the Spiritual Exercises," The
        Month, CLXVI, No. 855 (September),
        268-270.
235. Kelly, Bernard. The Mind & Poetry of
        Gerard Manley Hopkins, S.J. ("Stones
        from the Brook," No. 2.) London:
        Pepler & Sewell; unpaginated.
  236. R[ead], H[erbert]. in The Criterion, XV,
          No. 58 (October), 174.
  237. Vann, Gerald, O.P. in The Colosseum, II,
          No. 7 (September), 233-234.
238. Landier, Germain. "Lettres de Gérard
        Manley Hopkins," Mesures [Paris] , I,
        No. 1 (January 15), 103-109.
239. Leahy, Maurice. "Father Gerard Manley
        Hopkins, Jesuit and Poet," The Irish
        Monthly, IXIII (September), 567-576.
240. Maynard, Theodore. "When the Pie Was
        Opened," The Commonweal, XXII, No. 14,
        (August 2), 339-341.
241. New Verse, No. 14 [Gerard Manley Hopkins
        Issue] (April):
        Bremond, André, S. J. "Art and Inspira-
        tion," 5-12.

Devlin, Christopher, S.J. "Hopkins and
    Duns Scotus," 12-17.
Griffith, Ll. Wyn. "The Welsh Influence,"
    27-29.
Grigson, Geoffrey. "Blood or Bran," 21-
    23.
Grigson, Geoffrey. "Hopkins and Hopkinese,"
    24-26.
House, Humphry. "A Note on Hopkins's
    Religious Life," 3-5.
MacNeice, Louis. "A Comment," 26-27.
Madge, Charles. "What is All This
    Juice?" 17-21.
    242. T[urnell], G. M. in The Colosseum, II,
        No. 6 (June), 156-158.
243. Ogden, C. K. Editorial in Psyche [Camb-
    ridge: The Orthological Institute],
    XV, 5-18.
244. Plowman, Max. "Gerard Manley Hopkins,"
    The Adelphi, IX, No. 6 (March), 356-
    361.
245. Plowman, Max. Correspondence in The
    Times Literary Supplement (London),
    February 28, p. 124.
    [Query on Hopkins' birthdate.]
246. Roditi, Edouard. "Poèmes de Gerard
    Manley Hopkins," Mesures [Paris], I,
    No. 1 (January 15), 91-102.
247. Roggen, F. N. "Gerard Manley Hopkins,"
    Studies in English Literature [Im-
    perial University, Tokyo] , XV, 517-
    534.
248. Ryan, Sister Mary Phillip. O.P. Gerard
    Manley Hopkins: The Physical Basis
    of His Poetical Forms. Unpublished
    M.A. thesis, University of Detroit.
249. Sargent, Daniel. "Gerard Manley Hopkins,"
    Four Independents. New York: Sheed
    & Ward, Inc., pp. 117-183.

250. Stritch, Thomas John. Matter and Form in
        the Poetry of Gerard Manley Hopkins.
        Unpublished M.A. thesis, University of
        Notre Dame.
251. Young, G. M. "Tunes Ancient and Modern,"
        Life and Letters, XI, No. 62 (February),
        544-554.
252. Z[abel], M. D. "Hopkins in His Letters,"
        Poetry, XLVI, No. 4 (July), 210-219.

                            1936
[190-191]. Abbott, Clàude Colleer. The Corre-
        spondence of GMH and Richard
        Watson Dixon. The Letters of
        GMH to Robert Bridges. 1935.
  253. Cazamian, L. in Revue Anglo-Américaine,
        XIII (April), 349-350.
254. Arnold, Jerome Louis. A Study of Imagery
        in the Poetry of Gerard Manley Hopkins,
        S.J. Unpublished M.A. thesis, Univer-
        sity of Western Ontario.
255. Baldi, Sergio. "Cattolicesimo e Poesia
        nel 'Naufragio del Deutschland,'"
        Il Frontespizio [Rome], XI, No. 3
        (March), 154-164.
256. Barrett, Alfred, S.J. "Critics, Commu-
        nists and Gerard Manley Hopkins,"
        America, LVI, No. 4 (October 31), 90-
        91.
257. Basil, Sister M., O.S.F. "Gerard Manley
        Hopkins," Burnished Gold [College of
        St. Francis, Joliet, Illinois], I,
        62-67.
258. Clarke, Egerton. "Gerard Hopkins,
        Jesuit," The Dublin Review, CXCVIII,
        No. 396 (January-March), 227-241.

259. Daiches, David. "Gerard Manley Hopkins
     and the Modern Poets," New Literary
     Values: Studies in Modern Literature.
     London and Edinburgh: Oliver & Boyd,
     pp. 23-51.
260. Dimnet, Ernest. "Father Hopkins: The
     Poet Jesuit," The Pylon [Rome], III,
     No. 2 (April), 11-12.
261. Dohmann, Sister Ottilia. The Poetic
     Mind of Gerard Manley Hopkins, S.J.
     Unpublished Ph. D. dissertation,
     Fordham University.
262. Downey, Harris. "Gerard Hopkins: A
     Study of Influences," The Southern
     Review, I, No. 4 (Spring), 837-845.
263. Escobar, Mario. "'Rosa Mystica,'" Il
     Frontespizio, XI, No. 10 (October),
     23.
264. Feeney, Leonard. "Father Hopkins and
     Professor Abbott," America, LVI, No.
     3 (October 24), 68.
265. Fletcher, John Gould. "Gerard Manley
     Hopkins--Priest or Poet?" The
     American Review, VI, No. 3 (January),
     331-346.
266. Gardner, W. H. "A Note on Hopkins and
     Duns Scotus," Scrutiny, V, No. 1
     (June), 61-70.
267. Gardner, W. H. "The Wreck of the
     Deutschland," Essays and Studies
     [English Association, 1935], XXI,
     124-152.
268. Ginnekin, Jac. Van. "Barbarous in
     Beauty," Onze Taaltuin [Rotterdam],
     V, No. 3 (July), 65-73.
269. James, Stanley B. "Father Gerard Manley
     Hopkins, S.J.," The Sentinel of the
     Blessed Sacrament, XXXIX, No. 9
     (September), 467-470.

270. Kelly, Blanche Mary. The Well of English.
New York: Harper & Brothers, pp. 286-
290, et passim.
271. Kelly, Hugh. "Father Gerard Hopkins in
His Letters," Studies, XXV, No. 98
(June),239-252.
272. Leahy, Maurice. "A Priest-Poet: Father
Gerard Manley Hopkins, S.J.," The
Irish Ecclesiastical Record, 5th ser.,
XLVII (April), 355-368.
273. Matthew, David. Catholicism in England
from 1535-1935: The Portrait of A
Minority, Its Culture and Tradition.
London: Longmans, Green and Co., pp.
228-229.
274. Morley, Christopher. "'The Wreck of the
Deutschland,'" The Saturday Review of
Literature, XIV, No. 16 (August 15),
12.
275. Muñoz Rojas, José A. "Gerard Manley
Hopkins," Cruz y Raja [Madrid], No.
34 (January), pp. 107-118.
276. Ogden, C. K. Editorial in Psyche [Camb-
ridge: The Orthological Institute],
XVI, 5-50.
277. Read, Herbert. "Gerard Manley Hopkins,"
In Defense of Shelley & Other Essays.
London: William Heinemann Ltd., pp.
111-144.
278. Roberts, Michael. "Introduction," in
The Faber Book of Modern Verse.
London: Faber and Faber, pp. 3-5.
279. Rosten, Norman. The Prosody of Gerard
Manley Hopkins. Unpublished M.A.
thesis, New York University.
280. Shaw, James Gerard. Correspondence in
The Commonweal, XXV, No. 3 (November
13), 69-71.
[Reply to Fletcher, in The American
Review, January.]

281. Wilson, Howard A. Gerard Manley Hopkins'
      Prosody. Unpublished M.A. thesis,
      State College of Washington.
282. Yeats, W. B. "Introduction," in The
      Oxford Book of Modern Verse 1892-1935.
      New York: Oxford University Press, pp.
      xxxix-xl.
283. Young, G. M. "Forty Years of Verse,"
      The London Mercury and Bookman, XXV,
      No. 206 (December), 112-122.

                        1937
284. Abbott, C. Colleer. Correspondence in
      Notes and Queries, CLXXII, No. 12
      (March 20), 210.
285. Abbott, C. Colleer. Correspondence in
      The Times Literary Supplement (London),
      March 13, p. 188.
286. Berchmans, Sister Louise, S.N.D. Corre-
      spondence in America, LVI, No. 18
      (February 6), 425.
287. Cattaui, Georges. "Notes sur Gerard
      Manley Hopkins," Yggdrasill [Paris],
      I, No. 12 (March 25).
288. Croce, Benedetto. "Un Gesuita Inglese
      Poeta: Gerard Manley Hopkins," La
      Critica [Naples] , XXXV, No. 2
      (March 20), 81-100.
289. Dicus, Sister Mary Vivian. An Analysis
      of the Literary Importance of Gerard
      Manley Hopkins. Unpublished M.A.
      thesis, University of Wichita.
290. Durant, Rev. Albert, O.S.A. The Concept
      of God in the Poetry of Gerard Manley
      Hopkins. Unpublished M.A. thesis, The
      Catholic University of America.
291. Feeney, Leonard, S.J. Correspondence in
      America, LVI, No. 16 (January 23), 380.
      [Reply to F. B. Thornton in America,
      January 23.]

292. Gardner, W. H.   "The Religious Problem
      in G. M. Hopkins," Scrutiny, VI, No. 1
      (June), 32-42.
293. Gilkes, Martin.   "Gerard Manley Hopkins,
      Pioneer," A Key to Modern Poetry.
      London: Blackie & Son Limited, pp. 20-
      39.
294. Gordon, David.   Correspondence in America,
      LVI, No. 18 (February 6), 425.

      [Reply to F. B. Thornton in America,
      January 23.]
295. Groom, Bernard.   "The Formation and Use
      of Compound Epithets in English Poetry
      from 1579," S. P. E. [Society of Pure
      English], Tract No. XLIX, 318-320.
296. House, Humphry.   "Preface," The Note-
      Books and Papers of Gerard Manley
      Hopkins. London & New York: Oxford
      University Press, pp. xi-xxxvi.
297. Anon.   in The Springfield Republican
      [Massachusetts], February 28, p. 7.
298. Anon.   in The Tablet, CLXIX (February 6),
      198-200.
299. Anon.   in The Times Literary Supplement
      (London), January 23, p. 57.
300. Blackmur, R. P.   in The Virginia Quarterly
      Review, XIII, No. 3 (Summer), 449-453.
301. Cox, R. G.   in Scrutiny, V, No. 4 (March),
      455-456.
302. Day Lewis, C.   in Left Review, III, No.
      3 (April), 172-175.
303. De Selincourt, Basil.   in The Observer
      [London] , January 24, p. 5.
304. Deutsch, Babette, in New York Herald
      Tribune Books, May 16, p. 21.
305. Dobrée, Bonamy.   in The Spectator, CLVIII
      (March 12), 479-480.
306. Evans, B. Ifor.   in The Manchester
      Guardian, February 5, p. 7.
307. Feeney, Leonard.   in America, LVII, No. 2
      (April 17), 45-46.

308. Feeney, Leonard. in America, LVIII, No.
      9 (December 4), sec. 2, p. ii.
309. Flanner, Hildegarde. in The New Republic,
      XC (March 31), 243.
310. Forster, Leonard. in English Studies
      [Amsterdam], XIX, No. 5 (October),
      236-239.
311. Friend-Pereira, F. J. in The New Review
      [Calcutta] , VI (November), 473-475.
312. Holmes, John. in Boston Evening Tran-
      script, May 15, sec. 6, p. 1.
313. K[eating], J[oseph]. in The Month,
      CLXIX, No. 872 (February), 175-176.
314. K[elly], B[lanche] M[ary]. in The
      Catholic World, CXLV, No. 870
      (September), 750-751.
315. MacNeice, Louis. in The Criterion, XVI,
      No. 65 (July), 698-700.
316. Maude, Mother Mary, C.S.M. in The Living
      Church, XCVI, No. 16 (April 17), 495-
      496.
317. Moss, Ernest. in The Dublin Review, CCI,
      No. 402 (July), 165-167.
318. Muir, Edwin. in The London Mercury and
      Bookman, XXXV, No. 209 (March), 511-
      512.
319. Phillipson, Dom Wulstan. in The Downside
      Review, LV, No. 164 (October), 526-
      536.
320. Shuster, George N. in The Commonweal,
      XXVI, No. 6 (June 4), 164.
321. Stonier, G. W. in The New Statesman and
      Nation, XIII, No. 309 (January 23),
      124-126.
322. Troy, William. in The Nation, CXLIV, No.
      18 (May 1), 511-512.
323. Trueblood, Charles K. in Poetry, L, No.
      5 (August), 274-280.

324. Walker, M. E. in The New York Times Book Review, June 27, p. 6.
325. Whitridge, Arnold. in The Saturday Review of Literature, XVI, No. 11 (July 10), 20.
326. Kelly, Bernard. "Gerard Manley Tuncks," Blackfriars, XVIII, No. 207 (June), 424-429.
327. Kelly, Blanche Mary. "Immortal Diamond," The Catholic World, CXLIV, No. 867 (January),481-482. [Excerpt from The Well of English, 1936.]
328. McCrossan, Sister Joseph Marie, I.H.M. The Magic Baton of Gerard Manley Hopkins. Unpublished M.A. thesis, Villanova University.
329. MacManus, Francis. "Gerard Manley Hopkins, S.J.: I. Return of a Victorian," The Irish Monthly. LXV, No. 767 (May), 327-335; "II. The Poet Who Knew Too Much," No. 768 (June), 389-399.
330. Mansfield, Margery. Workers in Fire: A Book About Poetry. New York: Longmans, Green and Co., pp. 147-149, 161-165.
331. Noonan, James Joseph. Evidences of the Supernatural in the Poetry of Gerard Manley Hopkins. Unpublished M.A. thesis, Boston College.
332. Pompen, Fr. Aurelius, O.F.M. "Gerard Manley Hopkins, S.J.," Onze Taaltuin [Rotterdam], VI, No. 1 (May), 95-102.
333. Sheetz, Sister Mary Johannina. Gerard Manley Hopkins: A Modern Victorian. Unpublished M.A. thesis, Creighton University.
334. Simons, John W. "Hopkins in His Sermons," The Commonweal, XXVI, No. 24 (September 24), 491-493.

335. Thornton, Francis Beauchesne. "Gerard
Manley Hopkins: Major Poet or Major
Craftsman?" America, LVI, No. 16
(January 23), 379-380.
336. Thornton, Francis Beauchesne. "Hopkins
Again," America, LVI, No. 20 (February
20), 475.
337. Waterhouse, John F. "Gerard Manley
Hopkins and Music," Music and Letters,
XVIII, No. 3 (July), 227-235.
338. Weygandt, Cornelius. The Time of Yeats:
English Poetry of To-Day Against an
American Background. London: D.
Appleton-Century Company, Inc., pp.
386-388, et passim.
339. Willer, William Herman. The Poetic
Evolution of Gerard Manley Hopkins.
Unpublished M.A. thesis, University
of Minnesota.
340. Young, G. M. "Forty Years of Verse,"
Daylight and Champaign: Essays.
London: Jonathan Cape, pp. 189-206.
[Reprinted from The London Mercury
and Bookman, December, 1936.]

1938
[190-191]. Abbott, Claude Colleer. The
Correspondence of GMH and
Richard Watson Dixon, The Letters
of GMH to Robert Bridges, 1935.
341. Wild, Friedrich. in Beiblatt zur Anglia
[Tübingen], XLIX, No. 3 (March), 78-82.
342. Abbott, Claude Colleer. "Introduction,"
Further Letters of Gerard Manley
Hopkins including his Correspondence
with Coventry Patmore. London: Oxford University Press, pp. xix-xxxviii.
343. Anon. in The New Yorker, XIV, No. 19
(June 25), 67.

344. Anon. in The Tablet, CLXXI (May 21),
        666-667.
345. Anon. in The Times Literary Supplement
        (London), May 7, p. 312.
346. Bogan, Louise. in The Nation, CXLVII,
        No. 5 (July 30), 111-112.
347. Cox, R. G. in Scrutiny, VII, No. 2
        (September), 217-218.
348. Deutsch, Babette. in New York Herald
        Tribune Books, August 21, p. 12.
349. Dobrée, Bonamy. in The Spectator, CLX
        (May 13), 880.
350. Evans, B. Ifor. in The Manchester
        Guardian, June 24, p. 7.
351. Feeney, Leonard. in America, LX, No. 8
        (November 26), sec. 2, pp. x-xi.
352. Fitts, Dudley, in The Saturday Review of
        Literature, XVIII, No. 11 (July 9),
        15.
353. Gordon, David. in America, LIX, No. 24
        (September 17), 573-574.
354. H[arrold], C[harles] F. in Modern Phi-
        lology, XXXV, No. 4 (May), 440.
355. Holmes, John. in Boston Evening Tran-
        script, August 20, sec. 3, p. 1.
356. L'Estrange, H. K., S.J. in Blackfriars,
        XIX, No. 219 (June), 465-467.
357. [L'Estrange, H. K., S.J.]. in The Month,
        CLXXI, No. 888 (June), 569-570.
358. MacM[anus], F[rancis]. in The Irish
        Monthly, LXVI, No. 781 (July), 508-510.
359. Maude, Mother Mary, C.S.M. in The Living
        Church, XCIX, No. 10 (September 7),
        214.
360. M[eagher], M[argaret] C. in The Catholic
        World, CXLVII, No. 882 (September),
        758-759.
361. N., C. S. in The Oxford Magazine, LVI,
        No. 16 (March 10), 522-523.

362. Pick, John. in The Commonweal, XXVIII, No. 11 (July 8), 302-303.
363. Quinn, Kerker. in Poetry, LIII, No. 3 (December), 150-155.
364. Routh, H. V. in The Year's Work in English Studies, XIX, 243-244.
365. Stonier, G. W. in The New Statesman and Nation, n. s., XV, No. 377 (May 14), 840-842.
366. Walker, M. E. in The New York Times Book Review, July 10, p. 9.
367. Zabel, Morton Dauwen. in The New Republic, XCVII (November 30), 106.
368. Angus, Anne Margaret. "Gerard Manley Hopkins," The Canadian Poetry Magazine, III, No. 1 (June), 9-14.
369. Cochrane, Josephine M. Gerard Manley Hopkins: His Conception of Catholicism. Unpublished M.A. thesis, New York University.
370. Coogan, Marjorie D. "Dare-Gale Skylark," Fonthill Dial [College of Mount St. Vincent, New York, N. Y.], XIX, No. 4 (June), 12-19.
371. Daly, J. J., S.J. "Father Hopkins and the Society of Jesus," Thought, XIII, No. 48 (March), 9-13.
372. Gordon, David. "The Prose of Gerard Manley Hopkins," America, LIX, No. 15 (July 16), 355-356.
373. Hayes, George Michael. Gerard Manley Hopkins as a Critic. Unpublished M.A. thesis, University of Wisconsin.
374. Heywood, Terence. "Hopkins and Bridges on Trees," The Poetry Review, XXIX, No. 3 (May-June), 213-218.
375. Hughes, Emily. "The Innovators," The Irish Monthly, LXVI, No. 786 (December), 820-824.

376. James, Stanley B. "The Revolution in
      Literature," The Catholic Bookman, I,
      No. 11-12 (July-August), 386-388.
377. MacColl, D. S. "Patmore and Hopkins:
      Sense and Nonsense in English Prosody,"
      The London Mercury and Bookman, XXXVIII,
      No. 225 (July), 217-224.
378. MacKay, Ronald Dickie. Form in the Poetry
      of Gerard Manley Hopkins, Unpublished
      M.A. thesis, University of Toronto.
379. Panhuysen, Jos. "De Poezie van Gerard
      Manley Hopkins," Boekenschouw [Amster-
      dam], XXXII, No. 7 (November 15), 313-
      318.
380. Phillipson, Dom Wulstan. "Gerard Hopkins,
      Priest," The Downside Review, LVI, No.
      167 (July), 311-323.
381. Pick, John Francis. Religious Thought
      and Experience in the Poetry of Gerard
      Manley Hopkins. Unpublished Ph. D.
      dissertation, University of Wisconsin.
382. Read, Herbert Edward. "Gerard Manley
      Hopkins," Collected Essays in Literary
      Criticism. London: Faber and Faber
      Ltd., pp. 331-353.
383. Slater, John Rothwell. Recent Literature
      and Religion. New York: Harper &
      Brothers, pp. 185-189.
384   Srinivasa Iyengar, K. R. "Gerard Manley
      Hopkins," The New Review [Calcutta],
      VII (January), 1-11; (February), 115-
      125; (March), 264-273.
385. Turnell, Martin. Poetry and Crisis.
      London: Sands, The Paladin Press,
      pp. 26-27.
386. Walker, Ralph S. "An Introduction to
      the Poetry of Gerard Manley Hopkins,"
      The Aberdeen University Review, XXV,
      No. 75 (July), 232-243.

387. Williamson, C[laude] C. H. "Gerard
      Manley Hopkins," Pax, XXVIII, No. 201
      (July), 87-91; No. 202 (August), 107-
      110.

                    1939
[342]. Abbott, Claude Colleer. Further Letters
        of GMH including his Correspondence
        with Coventry Patmore. 1938.
388. Blackmur, R. P. in The Kenyon Review, I,
      No. 1 (Winter), 96-99.
389. Gregory, Horace. in The Yale Review,
      XXVIII, No. 2 (Winter), 415-418.
390. Leishman, J. B. in The Review of English
      Studies, XV, No. 58 (April), 243-246.
391. Phillipson, Dom Wulstan. in The Downside
      Review, LVII, No. 171 (July), 389-398.
392. Bailey, Ruth. A Dialogue on Modern
      Poetry. London: Oxford University
      Press, pp. 42-44, 61-65.
393. Binyon, Laurence. "Gerard Hopkins and
      His Influence," University of Toronto
      Quarterly, VIII, No. 3 (April), 264-
      270.
394. Brégy, Katherine. "Of Poets and Poetry,"
      The Catholic World, CXLVIII, No. 887
      (February), 522-530.
395. Burton, James. The Metrical Theory of
      Gerard Manley Hopkins. Unpublished
      M.A. thesis, University of Texas.
396. Castelli, Alberto. Scrittori Inglesi
      Contemporanei. Messina: Casa Editrice
      Giuseppe Principato, pp. 13-29.
397. Coogan, Margery D. The Nature Poetry of
      Gerard Manley Hopkins. Unpublished
      M.A. thesis, Catholic University of
      America.

398. Daly, James J. "One Way of Getting a
        Catholic Literature," Thought, XIV,
        No. 55 (December), 537-538.
399. D'Arcy, Rev. Martin, S.J. "Gerard
        Manley Hopkins," in Great Catholics,
        ed. Claude Williamson, O.S.C. New
        York: The Macmillan Company, pp.
        358-366.
400. Durand, Anthony Jospeh. The Metrical
        Theory of G. M. Hopkins. Unpublished
        M.A. thesis, University of Western
        Ontario.
401. Elliott, B. E. Gerard Manley Hopkins.
        Unpublished M.A. thesis, University
        of Western Australia.
402. The Ethos [Emmanuel College, Boston],
        XII, No. 2 (April): "Gerard Manley
        Hopkins, S.J.: A Poet for the
        Twentieth Century":
      Caliri, Flavia M. "His Inspiration,"
        71-75.
      Caulfield, Jeanne. "His Life," 75-78.
      Donovan, Mary. "His Message," 78-81.
403. Etman, Nol. "Haunting Rhythm,"
        Tijdschrift Voor Taal en Lettern
        [Amsterdam], XXVII (April), 94-101.
404. Finlay, Ida. "Gerard Manley Hopkins--
        Poet and Priest," The Cornhill
        Magazine, CLIX, No. 952 (April), 467-
        478.
405. Heffernan, Miriam Margaret. Gerard
        Manley Hopkins as Critic and Theorist
        of English Literature. Unpublished
        M.A. thesis, Columbia University.
406. Henderson, Philip. "Gerard Manley
        Hopkins," The Poet and Society.
        London: Martin Secker and Warburg,
        pp. 103-131.

407. Heywood, Terence. "Hopkins' Ancestry,"
      Poetry, LIV, No. 4 (July), 209-218;
      No. 5 (August), 271-279.
408. Heywood, Terence. "On Approaching
      Hopkins," The Poetry Review, XXX, No.
      3 (May-June), 185-188.
[296]. House, Humphry. The Note-Books and
      Papers of GMH. 1937.
      [389]. Gregory, Horace. in The Yale Review,
              XXVIII, No. 2 (Winter), 415-418.
409. Hughes, Emily. "The Innovators,"
      Catholic Digest, III, No. 3 (January),
      77-78.
      [On Hopkins and Debussy; condensed
      from The Irish Monthly, December, 1938.]
410. Jones, Glyn. "Hopkins and Welsh Prosody,"
      Life and Letters To-day, XXI, No. 22
      (June), 50-54.
411. Karp, Georg. Germanisches Formgefühl
      bei Gerard Manley Hopkins. Unpublish-
      ed Ph.D. dissertation, University of
      Marburg.
412. Kenmare, Dallas. "The Passionate Chris-
      tian: A Paper on Gerard Manley Hopkins,"
      The Face of Truth: Collected Writings
      on Poetry & Religion. Oxford: Shake-
      speare Head Press, pp. 92-100.
413. [Murray, John, S.J.]. Editorial in The
      Month, CLXXIII, No. 898 (April), 293-
      294.
414. Williams, Charles. "Gerard Manley
      Hopkins and Milton," The Poetry Review,
      XXX, No. 4 (July-August), 307-308.

                        1940
[342]. Abbott, Claude Colleer. Further Letters
      of GMH including his Correspondence
      with Coventry Patmore. 1938.

415. Bremond, André. in Etudes, CCXLII, No. 3
      (February 5), 310-317.
416. Abbott, Claude Colleer. "Gerard Manley
      Hopkins: A Letter and Drafts of Early
      Poems," The Durham University Journal,
      n. s., I, No. 1 (January), 65-73.
417. Applejoy, Petronius [D. R. Lock]. "Hopkins
      Sets a Poetic Signpost," The Catholic
      World, CLI, No. 902 (May), 184-190.
418. Baldi, Sergio. "Nota su una Traduzione
      da Hopkins," Letteratura: Rivista
      Trimestrale di Letteratura Contemporanea
      [Florence], IV, No. 2 (April-June),
      111-117.
419. Bardacke, Theodore Joseph. Gerard Manley
      Hopkins. Unpublished M.A. thesis,
      Syracuse University.
420. Barrett, Alfred, S.J. "Image Makers and
      Image Breakers," Spirit, VII, No. 3
      (July), 84-87.
421. Cox, Dorothy Scarborough. The Mind of
      Gerard Manley Hopkins. Unpublished
      M.A. thesis, University of Texas.
422. Daiches, David. "Thomas Hardy--A. E.
      Housman--Gerard Manley Hopkins,"
      Poetry and the Modern World. Chicago:
      University of Chicago Press, pp. 17-37.
423. Daly, James J., S.J. "Father Hopkins and
      the Society," The Jesuit in Focus.
      Milwaukee: The Bruce Publishing Com-
      pany, pp. 189-194.
424. Evans, Benjamin Ifor. "Towards the
      Twentieth Century: Gerard Manley
      Hopkins and T. S. Eliot," Tradition
      and Romanticism: Studies in English
      Literature from Chaucer to W. B. Yeats.
      London: Methuen & Co., Ltd., pp. 185-
      200.

425. Fraunces, John, S.J. The Meaning and
     Use of Inscape. Unpublished M.A.
     thesis, Loyola University [Chicago].
426. Heywood, Terence. "Gerard Manley Hopkins:
     His Literary Ancestry," English, III,
     No. 13 (Spring), 16-24.
427. Pick, John. "Growth of a Poet: Gerard
     Manley Hopkins," The Month, CXXXV,
     No. 907 (January), 39-46; No. 908
     (February), 106-113.
428. Saint Milo, Sister. The Sonnets of
     Gerard Manley Hopkins. Unpublished
     M.A. thesis, University of Montreal.
429. Southworth, James G. "Gerard Manley
     Hopkins," Sowing the Spring: Studies
     in British Poets from Hopkins to Mac -
     Neice. Oxford: Basil Blackwell, pp.
     15-32.
430. Weiss, Theodore. Gerard Manley Hopkins.
     Unpublished M.A. thesis, Columbia
     University.
431. Weiss, Theodore. "On Seeing a Portrait
     of Gerard Manley Hopkins," Columbia
     University Quarterly, XXXII, No. 4
     (December), 332.
432. Wells, Henry W. New Poets from Old: A
     Study in Literary Genetics. New York:
     Columbia University Press, pp. 35-43.

                    1941
433. Baldi, Sergio. Gerard Manley Hopkins.
     Brescia: Morcelliana; 263 pp.
434. Bernstein, Melvin Herbert. Nature and
     Pessimism in Gerard Manley Hopkins:
     A Study in Romantic Agony. Un-
     published M.A. thesis, New York
     University.

435. Cooney, Mother Madeleine Sophie. <u>A Study of Tone Color in the Poetry of Gerard Manley Hopkins, S.J.</u> Unpublished M.A. thesis, Marquette University.

436. Daly, James J. "Conscience Among the Books," <u>America</u>, LXVI, No. 3 (October 25), 73-74.

437. Dever, Joseph. "Gerard Manley Tuncks!" <u>The Stylus</u> [Boston College], LIV, No. 5 (March), 5-16.

438. Gardner, W. H. "G. Manley Hopkins as a <u>Cywyddwr</u>," <u>The Transactions of the Honourable Society of Cymmrodorion, 1940</u>, pp. 184-188.

439. Kite, Elizabeth S. "Conflict and Vision in Hopkins," <u>America</u>, LXV, No. 15, (July 19), 411-412.

440. Lind, L. Roberto. "Gerard Manley Hopkins: Poeta Menor de la Edad Mediavictoriana," <u>Universidad de la Habana</u>, No. 36-37 (May-August), pp. 48-55.

441. Matthai, A. P. "Hopkins the Jesuit," <u>The New Review</u> [Calcutta] , XIII, No. 4 (April), 306-317.

442. Matthiessen, F. O. <u>American Renaissance: Art and Experience in the Age of Emerson and Whitman</u>. New York: Oxford University Press, pp. 584-592. [On Hopkins and Whitman.]

443. Melody, Sister Winifred. <u>Gerard Manley Hopkins: Critic of English Poetry</u>. Unpublished M.A. thesis, University of Notre Dame.

444. Ong, Walter J., S.J. <u>Historical Backgrounds of Sprung Rhythm in Modern English Verse: A Preliminary Survey</u>. Unpublished M.A. thesis, St. Louis University.

445. Ronniger, Karl. Versuch einer Systematis-
     chen Ordnung der Metrischen Theorien
     Gerard Manley Hopkins. Unpublished
     Ph.D. dissertation, University of
     Vienna.
446. Speaight, Robert. "Gerard Manley Hopkins,
     S.J.," The Commonweal, XXXIII, No. 23,
     (March 28), 562-565.
447. Stanford, W. B. "Gerard Manley Hopkins
     and Aeschylus," Studies, XXX, No. 119
     (September), 359-368.
448. Sylvester, Howard E. A Study of Gerard
     Manley Hopkins. Unpublished M.A.
     thesis, University of New Mexico.
449. Whitridge, Arnold. "Gerard Manley
     Hopkins," University Review, VII, No.
     4 (June), 247-256.

                    1942
450. B[ell], D[avid]. "The Problem of Transla-
     tion," Y Cymmrodor [London] , XLVIII,
     63-103.
451. Engel, Monroe. Gerard Manley Hopkins:
     Inscapist Poet. Unpublished honors
     thesis, Harvard University.
452. Farrell, Sister Mary Pius. The Influence
     of the Liturgy on the Works of Gerard
     Manley Hopkins. Unpublished senior
     thesis, Manhattanville College.
453. Gardner, W. H. Gerard Manley Hopkins: A
     Study of Poetic Idiosyncrasy in Rela-
     tion to Poetic Tradition. Unpublished
     Ph.D dissertation, University of
     London.
454. Kerr, Marguerite M., R.S.C.J. Gerard
     Manley Hopkins: Aspects of His Po-
     etical Theory and Practice. Un-
     published M.A. thesis, University of
     Detroit.

455. Lamb, A. L. F. "Gerard Manley Hopkins,"
     The Central Literary Magazine, XXXVI,
     No. 1 (November), 50-55.
456. Leahy, Maurice. "'The Terrible Sonnets,'"
     The Voice [St. Mary's Seminary, Balti-
     more] , XIX, No. 4 (January), 19-20,
     35.
     [Summary of address by Leahy.]
457. Melchner, Sister Mary Roberta, S.S.N.D.
     Hopkins and the Common Man. Un-
     published M.A. thesis, Boston College.
458. O'Brien, Robert David, S.J. The Critical
     Mind of Gerard Manley Hopkins. Un-
     published M.A. thesis, Boston College.
459. Pick, John. Gerard Manley Hopkins:
     Priest and Poet. London: Oxford
     University Press; x, 169 pp.
     460. Anon. in The Durham University Journal,
           n. s., IV, No. 1 (December), 34-35.
     461. Anon. in The Listener, XXVIII, No. 722
           (November 12), 632, 635.
     462. Anon. in The Times Literary Supplement
           (London), September 26, p. 474.
     463. Conlay, Iris. in Catholic Herald [Lon-
           don], October 16, p. 3.
     464. F[aussett], H. I'A[nson]. in The Man-
           chester Guardian, October 7, p. 3.
     465. K., D. L. in The Month, CLXXVIII, No.
           930 (November-December), 493-494.
     466. Kelly, Hugh, S.J. in Studies, XXXI, No.
           124 (December), 438-444.
     467. Stonier, G. W. in The New Statesman and
           Nation, XXIV, No. 605 (September 26),
           207.
     468. Turnell, Martin. in The Tablet, CLXXX
           (October 17), 192.
     469. Turner, W. J. in The Spectator, CLXIX
           (October 2), 318.

470. Pick, John. "Gerard Manley Hopkins: The
     Problem of Religious Poetry," The
     Stylus [Boston College] , LV, No. 4
     (February), 14-22.
471. Sieveking, Lancelot. "Gerard Manley
     Hopkins," The Poetry Review, XXXIII,
     No. 5 (September-October), 323-325.
472. Taylor, Frajam. "The Rebellious Will of
     Gerard Manley Hopkins," Poetry, LIX,
     No. 5 (February), 270-278.
473. Tillemans, Th. "Is Hopkins a Modern
     Poet?" English Studies [Amsterdam],
     XXIV, No. 3 (June), 90-95.
474. Tobin, Sister Madeleine. The Literary
     Qualities in the Prose of Gerard
     Manley Hopkins. Unpublished M.A.
     thesis, University of Notre Dame.
475. Welch, Sister M. Charlotte, O.S.B. Unity
     of Gerard Manley Hopkins' Achievement.
     Unpublished M.A. thesis, Loyola Uni-
     versity [Chicago].

                    1943
476. Barry, Rev. John J. "Gerard Manley
     Hopkins," The Salesianum, XXXVIII, No.
     2 (April), 55-66.
477. [Casalandra], Sister M. Estelle, O.P.
     "The Blessed Virgin Compared to the
     Air We Breathe," The Rosary, XCIV,
     No. 10 (November), 16, 30.
478. Casalandra, Sister Estelle. Gerard
     Manley Hopkins: A Study in Spiritual
     Progress. Unpublished M.A. thesis,
     Ohio State University.
479. Colligan, Geraldine. "The Mysticism of
     Hopkins," The Ave Maria, n. s., LVIII,
     No. 19 (November 6), 591-593.
480. Darby, Harold S. "A Jesuit Poet--Gerard
     Manley Hopkins," The London Quarterly
     and Holborn Review, CLXVIII (April),
     110-122.

481. Gilman, William Henry. Gerard Manley
      Hopkins: The Man. Unpublished M.A.
      thesis, George Washington University.
482. Greene, Marjorie. "Immortal Diamond,"
      The Ethos [Emmanuel College, Boston],
      XVI, No. 3 (June), 127-132.
483. Holloway, Sister Marcella Marie. Gerard
      Manley Hopkins in the Light of Critical
      Opinion. Unpublished M.A. thesis,
      University of Missouri.
484. Kearney, Sister Mary Michael. Gerard
      Manley Hopkins, S.J. as Social Worker
      and Poet. Unpublished M.A. thesis,
      University of Vermont.
485. Lanctot, Sister Agnes. The Liturgical
      Concept of Life in Gerard Manley
      Hopkins and Paul Claudel. Unpublished
      M.A. thesis, University of Notre Dame.
486. Lilly, Gweneth. "The Welsh Influence in
      the Poetry of Gerard Manley Hopkins,"
      The Modern Language Review, XXXVIII,
      No. 3 (July), 192-205.
487. Mathison, John Kelly. The Poetical
      Relationship of Gerard Manley Hopkins,
      Coventry Patmore, and Francis Thompson.
      Unpublished Ph.D. disserationa, Prince-
      ton University.
488. Murphy, Sister Miriam Joseph. Gerard
      Manley Hopkins: Critic of his Con-
      temporaries in the Nineteenth Century.
      Unpublished M.A. thesis, University of
      Pittsburgh.
489. Nicol, B. De Bear. Correspondence in
      The Times Literary Supplement (London),
      May 13, p. 313.
      [On "The Windhover."]
490. Noon, W. T., S.J. Art Principles of
      Gerard Manley Hopkins, S.J. Unpublish-
      ed M.A. thesis, Loyola University
      [Chicago].

491. Parker, Mary. "Gerard Manley Hopkins:
      Poet of Design," Mount Mary Quarterly
      [Mount Mary College, Milwaukee], XIX,
      No. 2 (Winter), 21-34.
492. Pick, John. Correspondence in Catholic
      Book Club Newsletter, XXX, No. 3
      (June), 1-2.
      [Reply to R. W. Hanlon, in Catholic
      Book Club Newsletter, May.]
[459]. Pick, John. Gerard Manley Hopkins:
      Priest and Poet. 1942.
   493. Abbott, C. Colleer. in The Review of
         English Studies, XIX, No. 75 (July),
         311-313.
   494. Anon. in Notes and Queries, CLXXXV, No.
         8 (October 9), 240.
   495. Anon. in The Virginia Quarterly Review,
         XIX, No. 4 (Autumn), lxxxvi-lxxxvii.
   496. Ashburner, Phoebe. in The Adelphi, n. s.,
         XIX, No. 4 (July-September), 127-128.
   497. Baker, Carlos. in The New York Times
         Book Review, June 13, p. 10.
   498. Berryman, John. in The Harvard Advocate,
         CXXIX, No. 3 (March), 31-32.
   499. Carey, Charles M. in The Ave Maria,
         n.s., LVIII, No. 2 (July 10), 58.
   500. Deutsch, Babette. in The Nation, CLVII,
         No. 9 (August 28), 247.
   501. Eberhart, Richard. in Poetry, LXII, No.
         6 (September), 347-350.
   502. Gardiner, Harold C. in America, LXIX, No.
         16 (July 24), 439.
   503. Hanlon, R. W. in Catholic Book Club
         Newsletter, XXX, No. 2 (May), 1, 6.
   504. Hopkins, J. G. E. in Columbia, XXII, No.
         12 (July), 20.
   505. Lahey, Gerald F. in Thought, XVIII, No.
         71 (December), 721-722.

506. Lienhardt, R. G. in Scrutiny, XI, No. 3
     (Spring), 220-224.
507. Little, Arthur, S.J. in The Irish Monthly,
     LXXI, No. 836 (February), 47-59.
508. M[eagher], M[argaret]. in The Catholic
     World, CLVII, No. 940 (July), 439-441.
509. P., A. W. in The Downside Review, LX,
     No. 185 (January), 44.
510. P., E. S. in The Springfield Republican
     [Massachusetts], April 29, p. 8.
511. Shuster, George N. in The Saturday Re-
     view of Literature, XXVI, No. 23
     (June 5), 31.
512. Stephenson, A. A., S.J. in The Dublin
     Review, CCXII, No. 425 (April), 170-
     174.
513. T., C. in The Poetry Review, XXXIV, No.
     1 (January-February), 33-34.
514. Weyand, Norman, S.J. in The New World
     [Chicago], July 9, p. 11.
515. Weyand, Norman, S.J. in Books on Trial,
     II, No. 1 (May-June), 273.
516. Willy, Margaret. in English, IV, No. 22
     (Spring), 131-132.
517. Pick, John. "The Inspiration of Hopkins'
     Poetry," America, LXVIII, No. 16
     (January 23), 437-438.
518. Rose, Leslie. "Plumage of Far Wonder,"
     The Sentinel of the Blessed Sacrament,
     XLVI, No. 2 (February), 65-67.
     [On "The Wreck of the Deutschland."]
519. Scott, Rebecca Kathryn. The Individual-
     ism of Gerard Manley Hopkins. Un-
     published M.A. thesis, University of
     Missouri.

1944

520. Anderson, Mary Ann. "Fruit of Silence,"
The Mundelein College Review [Chicago],
XIV, No. 3 (May), 249-254.
521. Anon. "Gerard Manley Hopkins: 1844-1889,"
The Cholmeleian [Highgate School
Journal], LI, No. 306 (July), 741.
522. Anon. "Priest and Poet Gerard Hopkins
(1844-1889): The 'Dare-Gale Skylark,'"
The Times Literary Supplement (London),
June 10, pp. 282-284.
523. Benét, William Rose. "Centenary," The
Saturday Review of Literature, XXVII,
No. 36 (September 2), 28. [Poem.]
524. Bischoff, A., S.J. Correspondence in
America, LXXII, No. 2 (October 14), 39.
[Reply to Boyle, in America, September
30.]
525. Bliss, Geoffrey. "The Hopkins Centenary,"
The Month, CLXXX, No. 940 (July-
August), 233-240.
526. Boyle, Robert R., S.J. Correspondence
in America, LXXI, No. 26 (September
30), 623.
[Reply to Bischoff, in America,
September 2.]
527. Boyle, Robert R., S.J. "The Teaching of
Hopkins," Jesuit Educational Quarterly,
VII, No. 2 (October), 91-95.
528. Brooks, Cleanth. "Gerard Manley Hopkins,"
The Kenyon Review, VI, No. 3 (Summer),
321.
529. Brophy, Liam. "The Priest-Poet Who Elected
Silence," The Catholic Mirror, XXIV,
No. 8 (June), 14, 22.
530. Brophy, Liam. "Some Literary Centenaries
of Catholic Interest," The Irish
Catholic [Dublin], January 13, pp. 3-4.

531. Brown, Rev. Stephen J., S.J.   "A Catholic
      Approach to English Literature," The
      Irish Ecclesiastical Record, 5th ser.,
      LXIV, No. 6 (December), 368-377.
532. Burke, Sister Pauline, S.S.J.   The Wreck
      of the Deutschland. Unpublished M.A.
      thesis, Boston College.
533. Capellanus. Correspondence in America,
      LXX, No. 19 (February 12), 531.
      [Reply to Grady, in America, January
      29; on "The Windhover."]
534. [Casalandra], Sister M. Estelle, O.P.
      "The Tragedy of Gerald [sic] Manley
      Hopkins," The Rosary, XCV, No. 5 (May),
      21-24.
535. Cattaui, Georges. "Gerard Manley Hopkins,"
      Schweizer Rundschau [Einsiedeln],
      XLIV, No. 6 (September), 370-376.
536. Churchill, R. C. "Gerard Manley Hopkins:
      Christian Socialist," London Tribune,
      June 10.
537. D'Arcy, M. C., S.J.   "Gerard Manley
      Hopkins," The Tablet, CLXXXIII (June
      24), 308.
538. Davies, S. J. Correspondence in The
      Guardian [London] , August 25, p. 291.
      [Reply to Winstedt, in The Guardian,
      August 11.]
539. Davies, S. J.   "Gerard Manley Hopkins:
      'To What Serves Mortal Beauty?'" The
      Guardian [London], August 4, pp. 269-
      270.
      [Reply to Winstedt, in The Guardian,
      July 21.]
540. Ehmann, Rev. Benedict. "Father Gerard
      M. Hopkins, S.J.," Catholic Courier
      [Rochester, N. Y.], October 12, p. 15.

541. Ehmann, Rev. Benedict. "'Limber Liquid
      Youth,'" Catholic Courier [Rochester,
      N. Y.], October 26, p. 15.
542. Ehmann, Rev. Benedict. "The Poetry of
      Father Hopkins," Catholic Courier
      [Rochester, N. Y.], October 19, p. 15.
543. Gardner, W. H. Gerard Manley Hopkins:
      A Study of Poetic Idiosyncrasy in Rela-
      tion to Poetic Tradition. London:
      Martin Secker and Warburg, Ltd.; xvi,
      304 pp.
  544. Anon. in The Listener, XXXII (December
         21), 693-694.
  545. Anon. in The Times Literary Supplement
         (London), November 11, p. 550.
  546. H[ayes], J. J. in Studies, XXXIII, No.
         132 (December), 558-561.
  547. Lienhardt, R. G. in Scrutiny, XII, No.
         4 (Autumn), 296-301.
  548. Orwell, George. in The Observer [London],
         November 12, p. 3.
  549. Smalley, T., S.J. in Catholic Herald
         [London], November 24, p. 3.
  550. Stonier, G. W. in The New Statesman and
         Nation, November 4, pp. 307-308.
551. Grady, Rev. T. J. Poetic Principles of
      Gerard Manley Hopkins. Unpublished
      M.A. thesis, Loyola University
      [Chicago].
552. Grady, Thomas J. "Windhover's Meaning,"
      America, LXX, No. 17 (January 29),
      465-466.
553. Hanson, W. G. "Gerard Manley Hopkins and
      Richard Watson Dixon," The London
      Quarterly and Holborn Review, CXXXIII,
      No. 658 (January), 63-67.
554. Harding, H. W. "On First Looking into
      Gerard Manley Hopkins," The Poetry
      Review, XXXV, No. 2 (March-April), 77-
      78.

555. Hopkins, Gerard. Correspondence in The
     Times Literary Supplement (London),
     June 24, p. 309.
     [Note on Gerard Manley Hopkins'
     correct birthdate.]
556. House, Humphry. "Gerard Manley Hopkins:
     Poet-Priest," The Listener, XXXI, No.
     806 (June 22), 692-693.
557. Hughes, Emily. "Ripples on a Pool," The
     Irish Monthly, LXXII, No. 853 (July),
     280-285.
558. Jaworski, Sister M. C. Transcendent
     Victorianism of Gerard Manley Hopkins.
     Unpublished M.A. thesis, The Creighton
     University.
559. Kliger, Samuel. "God's Plenitude in the
     Poetry of Gerard Manley Hopkins,"
     Modern Language Notes, LIX, No. 6
     (June), 408-410.
560. Leavis, F. R. "Evaluations (IV): Gerard
     Manley Hopkins," Scrutiny, XII, No. 2
     (Spring), 82-93.
561. Lincoln, Eleanor. "Giving God Glory,"
     The Ariston [College of St. Catherine,
     St. Paul, Minnesota], XXXVIII, No. 3
     (June), 4-6.
562. Lowell, Robert. "A Note," The Kenyon
     Review, VI, No. 4 (Autumn), 583-586.
563. Maritain, Jacques. "Poetic Experience,"
     The Review of Politics, VI, No. 4
     (October), 387-402.
564. McLuhan, Herbert Marshall. "The Analogical
     Mirrors," The Kenyon Review, VI, No. 3
     (Summer), 322-332.
565. Miles, Josephine. "The Sweet and Lovely
     Language," The Kenyon Review, VI, No.
     3 (Summer), 355-368.

566. Mizener, Arthur. "Victorian Hopkins,"
     The Kenyon Review, VI, No. 4 (Autumn),
     590-606.
567. Moore, Dom Sebastian. "Gerard Manley
     Hopkins," The Downside Review, LXII,
     No. 190 (October), 184-195.
568. Pick, John. "The Centenary of Gerard
     Manley Hopkins," Thought, XIX, No. 75
     (December), 590-593.
[459]. Pick, John. Gerard Manley Hopkins:
     Priest and Poet. 1942.
   569. MacGillivray, Arthur, S.J. in Poet Lore,
        L, No. 3 (Autumn), 276-278.
570. Price, Fanny. "G. M. Hopkins on Robert
     Bridges," Notes and Queries, CLXXXVI,
     No. 2 (January 15), 49.
571. Reid, J. C. Gerard Manley Hopkins, Priest
     and Poet: A Centennial Tribute.
     (Catholic Writers' Movement Pamphlet.)
     Wellington, New Zealand: Catholic
     Supplies, Ltd.; 16 pp.
572. Ridler, Anne. "Gerard Hopkins," The
     Periodical [Oxford], XXVI, No. 210
     (July), 109-113.
573. Ruggles, Eleanor. Gerard Manley Hopkins:
     A Life. New York: W. W. Norton &
     Company, Inc.; viii, 305 pp.
   574. Abel, Darrel. in The South Atlantic
        Quarterly, XLIII, No. 4 (October),
        415-417.
   575. Anon. in Catholic Book Club Newsletter,
        XXXII, No. 5 (September), unpaginated.
   576. Anon. in The New Yorker, XX, No. 26
        (August 12), 64.
   577. Anon. in Time, XLIV, No. 7 (August 14),
        99-104.
   578. Auden, W. H. in The New Republic, CXI,
        No. 8 (August 21), 223-224.

579. Bischoff, A. in Ameriça, LXXI, No. 22
     (September 2), 539-540.
580. Currier, Isabel. in Boston Traveller,
     August 2.
581. Engle, Paul. in Chicago Sunday Tribune
     Books, July 30, p. 11.
582. Furness, Clifton Joseph. in The Atlantic
     Monthly, CLXXIV, No. 4 (October), 131-
     133.
583. Gregory, Horace. in New York Herald
     Tribune Weekly Book Review, August 6,
     p. 5.
584. H., R. B. in Orate Fratres, XIX, No. 1
     (December 3), 47-48.
585. Hughes, Riley. in Books on Trial, III,
     No. 4 (October-November), 617.
586. Kennedy, Leo. in The Chicago Sun Book
     Week, August 13, p. 9.
587. McLuhan, Herbert Marshall. in The New
     York Times Book Review, September 3,
     pp. 7, 14.
588. [O'Brien, Robert David]. in The Boston
     Globe, August 16, p. 15.
589. Pick, John. in The Commonweal, XL, No.
     19 (August 25), 447-448.
590. Sale, William M., Jr. in Poetry, LXV,
     No. 111 (December), 142-149.
591. Spencer, Theodore. in The Saturday
     Review of Literature, XXVII, No. 36
     (September 2), 20.
592. Varley, Lee. in The Springfield
     Republican [Massachusetts], October
     8, p. 4.
593. Warren, Austin. in The Kenyon Review,
     VI, No. 4 (Autumn), 587-589.
594. Weyand, Norman, S.J. in The New World
     [Chicago], September 15, p. 13.

595. Schoder, Raymond V. "Spelt from Sibyl's Leaves," Thought, XIX, No. 75 (December), 633-648.

596. Shaw, J. G. "Oddities and Obscurities," The Canadian Register, October 28, p. 8.

597. Shaw, J. G. "A Pilloried Poet," The Canadian Register, October 14, p. 5.

598. Shewring, Walter. "Gerard Manley Hopkins: 1844-1944," The Weekly Review [London], XL, No. 10 (November 30), 115-116.

599. Thomas, Marie A. "Gerard Manley Hopkins: 1844-1944," The Ethos [Emmanuel College, Boston], XVII, No. 3 (June), 142-153.

600. Thornton, Francis Beauchesne. "Essay on 'The Wreck of the Deutschland,'" The Catholic World, CLX, No. 955 (October), 41-46.

601. Turner, Vincent, S.J. "Gerard Manley Hopkins, 1844-1944," The Dublin Review, CCXV, No. 431 (October), 144-159.

602. Turner, W. J. "Gerard Manley Hopkins (1844 to 1889)," The Spectator, CLXXIII (July 14), 32-33.

603. [Van de Water, Charlotte]. "The Windhover," Scholastic, XLIV, No. 6 (March 13-18), 20.

604. Warren, Austin. "Instress of Inscape," The Kenyon Review, VI, No. 3 (Summer), 369-382.

605. Whitehall, Harold. "Sprung Rhythm," The Kenyon Review, VI, No. 3 (Summer), 333-354.

606. Winstedt, R. O. Correspondence in The Guardian [London], August 11, p. 276. [Reply to Davies in The Guardian, August 4.]

607. Winstedt, Sir Richard. "Gerard Manley Hopkins," The Guardian [London], July 21, p. 251.

1945

608. Brauns, M., S.J. "De Dichter Gerard
     Manley Hopkins, S.J.," Streven
     [Brussels], XII, No. 4 (August), 239-
     247.
609. Bremond, André. "La Poésie Naïve et
     Savante de Gérard Hopkins" and
     "Quelques Réflexions sur la Poésie et
     les Styles Poétiques," Le Charme et La
     Raison. Le Puy: Editions Xavier
     Mappas, pp. 49-86; 95-105.
610. Brown, Sister Margaret Eugene, C.S.J.
     Gerard Manley Hopkins: Literary
     Critic. Unpublished M.A. thesis,
     Saint John's University.
611. Delaney, Sister Anne Cyril, S.N.D. de
     Namur. The Christocentricity of
     Gerard Manley Hopkins. Unpublished
     M.A. thesis, Boston College.
[543]. Gardner, W. H. GMH: A Study of Poetic
     Idiosyncrasy in Relation to Poetic
     Tradition. 1944.
     612. D'Arcy, M. C. in The Month, CLXXXI, No.
          943 (January-February), 67-69.
     613. Gregory, Horace. in The Saturday Review
          of Literature, XXVIII, No. 12 (March
          24), 38-39.
     614. Hield, Robert. in The Daily Telegraph
          and Morning Post [London], January 5,
          p. 3.
     615. Kelly, Bernard. in Blackfriars, XXVI,
          No. 303 (June), 233-234.
     616. Pick, John. in Thought, XX, No. 77 (June)
          347-349.
     617. W., D. in The Tablet, January 13, p. 22.
     618. Williams, Charles. in Time & Tide, XXVI,
          No. 5 (February 3), 102-103.
     619. Willy, Margaret. in English, V, No. 28
          (Spring), 126-127.

620. Holloway, Roberta. Some Effects of
      Classical Study in the Work of Hopkins.
      Unpublished Ph.D. dissertation, Uni-
      versity of California [Berkeley].
621. Howarth. R. G. "Yeats and Hopkins,"
      Notes and Queries, CLXXXVIII, No. 10
      (May 19), 202-204.
622. The Kenyon Critics. Gerard Manley Hopkins.
      (The Makers of Modern Literature.)
      Norfolk, Connecticut: New Directions
      Books; viii, 144 pp.
      Leavis, F. R. "Metaphysical Isolation,"
      115-134.
      Lowell, Robert. "Hopkins' Sanctity,"
      89-93.
      McLuhan, Herbert Marshall. "The Ana-
      logical Mirrors," 15-27.
      Miles, Josephine. "The Sweet and Lovely
      Language," 55-71.
      Mizener, Arthur. "Victorian Hopkins,"
      94-114.
      Warren, Austin. "Gerard Manley Hopkins
      (1844-1889)," 1-14.
      Warren, Austin. "Instress of Inscape,"
      72-88.
      Whitehall, Harold. "Sprung Rhythm," 28-
      54.
623. Leahy, Maurice. "Laureate and Levite:
      Father Gerard Manley Hopkins, S.J.,
      Convert to the Church," The Epistle,
      XI, No. 1 (Winter), 12-14.
624. L[eyris], P[ierre]. "Putride Pature,"
      Dieu Vivant [Paris], No. 3, pp. 53-59.
625. Macri, Clare Grace. Gerard Manley Hopkins
      and Robert Bridges. Unpublished M.A.
      thesis, Columbia University.

626. Muñoz Rojas, José A. "En el Centenario
      de Gerard Manley Hopkins, S.J.,"
      Razón y Fe, CXXXII, No. 7 (November),
      569-574.
627. Noon, William T. "Hopkins: Christian
      Humanist," America, LXXIV, No. 3
      (October 20), 73-75.
[573]. Ruggles, Eleanor. Gerard Manley
      Hopkins: A Life. 1944.
      628. Harrold, Charles Frederick. in Journal
            of English and Germanic Philology,
            XLIV, No. 4 (October), 434-436.
      629. Kirschbaum, Leo. in Modern Language
            Notes, LX, No. 3 (March), 199-201.
      630. Lowell, Robert. in The Sewanee Review,
            LIII, No. 1 (Winter), 136-139.
631. Weiss, T. "The Apprenticeship of Gerard
      Manley Hopkins," in Selections from
      the Note-Books of Gerard Manley Hopkins.
      (The Poets of the Year.) Norfolk,
      Connecticut: New Directions; un-
      paginated.
632. Weiss, T. "Gerard Manley Hopkins:
      Realist on Parnassus," Accent, V, No.
      3 (Spring), 135-144.

                    1946
633. Baldi, Sergio. Correspondence in
      Anglica: Rivista di Studi Inglesi e
      Americani [Florence], I, No. 5
      (October), 211-212.
      [Reply to Guidi, in Anglica, October]
634. Carlson, Sister Marian Raphael, S.H.N.
      Gerard Manley Hopkins and His Work.
      Unpublished M.A. thesis, Loyola Uni-
      versity [Chicago].
635. Cohen, Selma Jean. The Poems of Gerard
      Manley Hopkins in Relation to His
      Religious Thought. Unpublished Ph.D.
      dissertation, University of Chicago.

636. Connolly, Francis X. "Reaffirmations of
      Poetic Values," Spirit, XIII, No. 2
      (May), 52-57.
637. Curran, Mary Doyle. A Commentary on the
      Poetry of Gerard Manley Hopkins. Un-
      published Ph.D. dissertation, Uni-
      versity of Iowa.
638. Devlin, Christopher. "An Essay on
      Scotus," The Month, CLXXXII, No. 954
      (November-December), 456-466.
639. Feeney, Leonard. "Oddity and Obscurity
      in Hopkins," From the Housetops, I,
      No. 2 (December), 24-29.
640. Gordon, George. "Gerard Manley Hopkins
      and Robert Bridges," The Discipline
      of Letters. Oxford: Clarendon Press,
      pp. 168-184.
641. Guidi, Augusto. "Problemi di Inter-
      pretazione in G. M. Hopkins," Anglica:
      Rivista di Studi Inglesi e Americani
      [Florence], I, No. 5 (October), 208-
      211.
[622]. The Kenyon Critics. Gerard Manley
        Hopkins. 1945.
    642. Anon. in The New Yorker, XXII, No. 2
          (February 23), 90-91.
    643. Anon. in The United States Quarterly
          Book List, II, No. 3 (September),
          171-172.
    644. Deutsch, Babette. in New York Herald
          Tribune Weekly Book Review, March 17,
          p. 12.
    645. Duffy, John, C.S.S.R. in Spirit, XIII,
          No. 3 (July), 88-91.
    646. Grady, Rev. Thomas J. in Books on Trial,
          V, No. 2 (July-August), 61.
    647. K., L. in The Chicago Sun Bookweek,
          February 3, sec. 5, p. 2.

648. Mack, Maynard. in The Yale Review, XXXV,
      No. 3 (Spring), 539-542.
649. Meagher, Margaret. in The Catholic World,
      CLXIII, No. 974 (May), 181-182.
650. Pick, John. in America, LXXIV, No. 20
      (February 16), 539.
651. Schwartz, Delmore. in The Nation, CLXII
      (March 23), 347-348.
652. Wyatt, E. V. R. in The Commonweal, XLIV,
      No. 1 (April 19), 20-21.
653. Lloyd Thomas, M. G. "Hopkins as Critic,"
      Essays and Studies [English Association,
      1945], XXXII, 61-73.
654. Maguire, Alice Marie. A Study of the
      Poetry of Gerard Manley Hopkins. Un-
      published M.A. thesis, Brown Univer-
      sity.
655. Minten, Sister Grace Ellen, O.P. The
      Literary Reputation of Gerard Manley
      Hopkins. Unpublished M.A. thesis,
      DePaul University.
656. Molloy, Eugene Joseph. The True Humanism
      of Gerard Manley Hopkins. Unpublished
      M.A. thesis, Saint John's University.
657. Sargent, Daniel. "Gerard Manley Hopkins,"
      From the Housetops, I, No. 1 (September),
      12-21.
658. Spehar, Elizabeth Marie. Gerard Manley
      Hopkins as a Literary Critic. Un-
      published M.A. thesis, University of
      Colorado.
659. Treece, Henry. "Gerard Manley Hopkins
      and Dylan Thomas," How I See Apoca-
      lypse. London: Lindsay Drummond,
      pp. 129-139.

660. Weiss, T. "Gerard Manley Hopkins:
     Realist on Parnassus," in Accent
     Anthrology, ed. Kerker Quinn and
     Charles Shattuck. New York: Harcourt,
     Brace and Company, pp. 664-677.
     [Reprinted from Accent, 1945].
[631]. Weiss, T. Selections from the Note-
     Books of GMH. 1945.

     661. Miller, A. J., S.J. in The Catholic
          Library World, XVII, No. 4 (January),
          128.
     662. Pick, John. in Thought, XXI, No. 80
          (March), 159-160.

                      1947
663. Anon. "Newly Discovered Journals of Fr.
     G. M. Hopkins," Letters and Notices,
     LV, No. 295 (May), 103-104.
664. Brooke-Rose, Christine. "La Syntaxe et
     le Symbolisme dans la Poésie de
     Hopkins," Europe [Paris] , XXV, No.
     19 (July), 30-39.
665. Cattaui, Georges. "Gerard Manley Hopkins
     ou Un Nouveau Lyrisme Baroque," Trois
     Poètes: Hopkins, Yeats, Eliot.
     Paris: Egloff, pp. 11-44.
666. Cohen, Selma Jeanne. "The Poetic Theory
     of Gerard Manley Hopkins," Philological
     Quarterly, XXVI, No. 1 (January), 1-20.
667. Collins, James. "Philosophical Themes in
     G. M. Hopkins," Thought, XXII, No. 84
     (March), 67-106.
668. Cranny, Titus. "Father Gerard Manley
     Hopkins: Poet of the King," The
     Magnificat, LXXX, No. 5 (September),
     251-258.

669.   D'Arcy, M[artin]C., S.J. The Mind and
       Heart of Love. New York: Henry Holt
       and Company, pp. 158-162, et passim.

670.   Eliott, Brian. "Gerard Hopkins and
       Marcus Clarke," Southerly [English
       Association, Sydney, Australia], VIII,
       No. 4, 218-227.

671.   Faussett, Hugh I'Anson. "Gerard Hopkins:
       A Centenary Tribute" and "The Conflict
       of Priest and Poet in Hopkins," Poets
       and Pundits: Essays and Addresses.
       London: Jonathan Cape, pp. 96-103;
       104-113.

672.   Ghiselin, Brewster. "Reading Sprung
       Rhythms," Poetry, LXX, No. 2 (May),
       86-93.

673.   Gibson, William M. "Hopkins' 'To R. B.,'"
       The Explicator, VI, No. 2 (November),
       item 12.

674.   Greene, Sister Moira. The Poetic Theory
       of Gerard Manley Hopkins and its
       Relation to his Own Work. Unpublished
       M.A. Thesis, University of Notre Dame.

675.   Guidi, Augusto. Il Naufragio del Deutsch-
       land, La Fine Dell' Euridice: Testo
       inglese Premessa e traduzione.
       Brescia: Morcelliana; 54 pp.

676.   Guidi, Augusto. Poeti Cattolici: Dell'
       Inghilterra Moderna. Rome: La Spiga,
       pp. 70-75.

677.   Holloway, Sister Marcella Marie. The
       Prosodic Theory of Gerard Manley
       Hopkins. Washington, D. C.: The
       Catholic University of America Press;
       121 pp.

678.   Howarth, R. G. "Hopkins and Sir Thomas
       More," Notes and Queries, CXCII, No.
       18 (September 6), 389.

679. Howarth, R. G. "Hopkins's Earlier Poems:
     The Order of Composition," Notes and
     Queries, CXCII, No. 12 (June 14),
     255-256.
[622]. The Kenyon Critics. Gerard Manley
       Hopkins. 1945.
    680. Harding, John Paul. in Liturgical Arts,
         XV, No. 2 (February), 50.
    681. Mowrer, Deane. in The New Mexico Quarter-
         ly Review, XVII, No. 3 (Autumn), 383-
         385.
682. Madeleva, Sister M., C.S.C. "What Shall
     I Sing?" Spirit, XIV, No. 3 (July),
     80-86.
     [From an address presented by The
     Catholic Poetry Society of America, at
     Manhattanville College of the Sacred
     Heart, New York City, March 16.]
683. Mandelbaum, Alice. Of Mind and Metaphor:
     A Study in Richard Crashaw and Gerard
     Manley Hopkins. Unpublished M.A.
     thesis, Columbia University.
684. Mathison, John K. "The Poetic Theory of
     Gerard Manley Hopkins," Philological
     Quarterly, XXVI, No. 1 (January), 21-
     35.
685. Mooney, Margaret Elizabeth. Gerard
     Manley Hopkins and Vincent Van Gogh.
     Unpublished M.A. thesis, Columbia
     University.
686. Purcell, J. M. "The Poetry of Gerard
     Manley Hopkins," Cronos, I, No. 2
     (Summer), 21-25.
687. Ruggles, Eleanor. Gerard Manley Hopkins:
     A Life. Second edition. London:
     John Lane; viii, 247 pp.
    688. Lynd, Robert. in The Observer [London],
         November 30, p. 3.

689. Trower, Philip. in The Spectator, CLXXIX
(December 19), 776-778.
690. Schneider, Elisabeth. "Hopkins' 'My Own
Heart Let Me Have More Pity On,'" The
Explicator, V, No. 7 (May), item 51.
691. Schwartz, Joseph M. Gerard Manley Hopkins
as Literary Critic: with Specific
Reference to the Criticism of hiᴜ
Significant Contemporaries as Seen in
his Correspondence. Unpublished M.A.
thesis, Marquette University.
692. Silverstein, Henry. "On 'Tom's Garland,'"
Accent, VII, No. 2 (Winter), 67-81.
693. Tindall, William York. Forces in Modern
British Literature: 1885-1946. New
York: Alfred A. Knopf, Inc., pp. 212-
216, et passim.
[631]. Weiss, T. Selections from the Note-
Books of GMH. 1945.
[680]. Harding, John Paul. in Liturgical Arts,
XV, No. 2 (February), 50.
[681]. Mowrer, Deane. in The New Mexico
Quarterly Review, XVII, No. 3
(Autumn), 383-385.
694. Wiles, Sister M. Peter. An Annotated
Edition of Selected Poems of Gerard
Manley Hopkins. Unpublished M.A.
thesis, Canisius College.

1948
695. Behn, Irene. Gerard Manley Hopkins:
Gedichte, Übertragung, Einführung und
Erlaüterung. Hamburg: Claassen &
Goverts; 144 pp.
[665]. Cattaui, Georges. Trois Poètes:
Hopkins, Yeats, Eliot. 1947.
696. Slocombe, George. in New York Herald
Tribune [European Edition: Paris],
December 1, p. 7.

697. Cocking, J. M. Correspondence in The
      Times Literary Supplement (London),
      July 31, p. 429.
      [Reply to Anon., in TLS, July 10.]
698. Doyle, Louis F. "To M'sieu Jourdain,"
      America, LXXIX, No. 24 (September 18),
      541-543.
699. Fitzgerald, Sister Marie Christine, G.N.
      S.H. The Influence of St. John of
      the Cross on Several Poets of the
      Victorian Era. Unpublished M.A.
      thesis, The Catholic University of
      America.
700. Gardner, W. H. Gerard Manley Hopkins
      (1844-1889): A Study of Poetic Idio-
      syncrasy in Relation to Poetic Tradi-
      tion. Second edition. London:
      Martin Secker and Warburg, I; xvi,
      304 pp.
    701. Anon. in The New Yorker, XXIV, No. 32
          (October 2), 102.
    702. Gardiner, Harold C. in America, LXXX,
          No. 6 (November 13), sec. 2, p. xxx.
    703. McKenzie, Gordon. in San Francisco
          Chronicle, "This World" supplement,
          September 26, p. 19.
    704. Meagher, Edward F. in The Commonweal,
          XLVIII, No. 21 (September 3), 505.
    705. Pearson, Norman Holmes. in The Saturday
          Review of Literature, XXXII, No. 38
          (September 17), 16-17.
    706. Pearson, Norman Holmes. in The Saturday
          Review of Literature, XXXII, No. 44
          (October 30), 26-27.
    707. Pick, John. in The Catholic World,
          CLXVIII (October), 90-91.

708. Gardner, W. H. "Introduction to the
          Third Edition," Poems of Gerard Manley
          Hopkins. Third edition. New York &
          London: Oxford University Press,
          pp. xiii-xxvi.

[702]. Gardiner, Harold C. in America, LXXX,
          No. 6 (November 13), sec. 2, p. xxx.

709. H[ayes], J. J. in Studies, XXXVII, No.
          148 (December), 494-497.

710. McDonald, Gerald. in Library Journal,
          LXXIII, No. 16 (September 15), 1277.

[704]. Meagher, Edward F. in The Commonweal,
          XLVIII, No. 21 (September 3), 505.

711. Pick, John. in America, LXXX, No. 1
          (October 9), 19.

[675]. Guidi, Augusto. Il Naufragio del
          Deutschland, La Fine Dell' Euridice.
          1947.

712. Anon. in La Civiltà Cattolica, XCIX
          (September 4), 529-530.

713. Haven, Richard. The Experience of Gerard
          Manley Hopkins: A Contextualist
          Approach to his Poetry. Unpublished
          honors thesis, Harvard University.

[677]. Holloway, Sister Marcella Marie. The
          Prosodic Theory of Gerard Manley
          Hopkins. 1947.

714. Gleeson, William F. in Thought, XXIII,
          No. 89 (June), 342-343.

[709]. H[ayes], J. J. in Studies, XXXVII, No.
          148 (December), 494-497.

715. Haddakin, Lilian. in The Modern Lan-
          guage Review, XLIII, No. 4 (October),
          534-535.

716. Howarth, R. G. "Hopkins--A Correction,"
     Notes and Queries, CXCIII, No. 7
     (April 3), 150.
     [The "correction" refers to a change
     suggested by Humphry House in The
     Note-Books and Papers of GMH. In a
     note printed here, House agrees with
     Howarth.]
717. Kenmare, Dallas. "The Hid Battlements,"
     The Poetry Review, XXXIX, No. 2
     (April-May), 199-207.
718. McNamara, Anne. A Study of Voice and
     Address in the Poetry of Gerard
     Manley Hopkins. Unpublished M.A.
     thesis, The Catholic University of America.
719. Melchiori, Giorgio. "Poeti Cattolici in
     Inghilterra," La Fiera Letteraria
     [Milan], III, No. 12 (March 28), 4.
720. Mims, Edward. "Gerard Manley Hopkins:
     Jesuit Scholar," The Christ of the
     Poets. Nashville, Tennessee:
     Abingdon-Cokesbury Press, pp. 204-211.
721. Peters, W. A. M., S.J. Gerard Manley
     Hopkins: A Critical Essay Towards
     the Understanding of his Poetry.
     London: Oxford University Press;
     xviii, 213 pp.
     722. Anon. in The Durham University Journal,
          n. s., IX, No. 3 (June), 98-99.
     723. Anon. in The Listener, XL (September
          30), 495-496.
     724. Anon. in The Times Literary Supplement
          (London), July 10, p. 386.
     725. F[aussett], H. I'A[nson]. in The Man-
          chester Guardian, April 13, p. 3.
     726. F[aussett], H. I'A[nson]. in The Man-
          chester Guardian Weekly, April 22,
          p. 10.

80   GERARD MANLEY HOPKINS

727. Grisewood, Harman. in <u>The Dublin Review</u>,
      CCXXI, No. 444 (Winter), 163-165.
[709]. H[ayes], J. J. in <u>Studies</u>, XXXVII, No.
      148 (December), 494-497.
[715]. Haddakin, Lilian. in <u>The Modern Lan-
      guage Review</u>, XLIII, No. 4 (October),
      534-535.
728. McCarthy, Desmond. in <u>Chicago Sun Book
      Week</u>, May 16, p. 10.
729. Morgan, William. in <u>The New English Re-
      view</u> [London], XVI, No. 6 (June),
      570-572.
730. Trethowan, Dom Illtyd. in <u>The Downside
      Review</u>, LXVI, No. 206 (October), 479.
731. Turner, Vincent, S.J. in <u>The Tablet</u>,
      CXCII (July 3), 10.
732. Pietrkiewicz, Jerzy. "Introducing
      Norwid," <u>The Slavonic and East Euro-
      pean Review</u>, XXVII, No. 68 (December),
      228-247.
      [Compares the Polish poet, Cyprian
      Norwid, and Hopkins.]
733. Roberts, Donald A. <u>The Technical Influ-
      ence of Gerard Manley Hopkins in
      Modern British Poetry</u>. Unpublished
      M.A. thesis, Columbia University.
[687]. Ruggles, Eleanor. <u>Gerard Manley
      Hopkins: A Life</u>. 1947.
734. Anon. in <u>The Times Literary Supplement</u>,
      (London), January 3, p. 11.
735. Clarke, Austin. in <u>The Irish Times</u>
      [Dublin], February 28, p. 4.
736. Grisewood, Harman. in <u>The Dublin Review</u>,
      CCXXI, No. 442 (Spring), 168-171.
737. K[elly], H[ugh]. in <u>Studies</u>, XXXVII, No.
      145 (March), 111-112.
738. Turner, Vincent, S.J. in <u>The Tablet</u>,
      CXCI (January 24), 58.

739. Ryan, Francis. "'The Wreck of the
     Deutschland': An Introduction and a
     Paraphrase," The Dublin Review, CCXXI,
     No. 443 (Autumn), 124-141.
740. Sharpe, Garold. Gerard Manley Hopkins:
     The Dublin Years. Unpublished M.A.
     thesis, Columbia University.
741. Sharper, Philip Jenkins, S.J. Evidences
     of the Mystical State in the "Terrible
     Sonnets" of Gerard Manley Hopkins.
     Unpublished M.A. thesis, Fordham Uni-
     versity.
742. Shea, Dennis Donald David. An Organiza-
     tion of Gerard Manley Hopkins' Critical
     Opinions. Unpublished M.A. thesis,
     Columbia University.
743. Simpson, Ruth Winifrid. Gerard Manley
     Hopkins: Religion and the Creative
     Process. Unpublished M.A. thesis,
     Duke University.
744. Smith, H. R. A Study of the Treatment of
     Nature in the Poetry of Gerard Manley
     Hopkins. Unpublished M.A. thesis,
     Ohio University.
745. Spheres [Mount St. Agnes College, Balti-
     more], (Gerard Manley Hopkins Issue.)
     Spring:
     Cunningham, Margaret. "Hopkins and
     Prosody," 10-13.
     DeLargy, Peggy, and Margaret Cunningham.
     "Hopkins and Analysis: 'Pied Beauty,'"
     5-6.
     DeLargy, Peggy. "Hopkins and Prose,"
     7-9.
     Eder, Betty. "Bibliography," 26-35.
     Evelyn, Sister Mary, R.S.M. "Hopkins and
     Theology," 22-24.
     Hohman, Janet. "Hopkins and History,"
     14-16.
     Miller, Nancy Lou. "Hopkins and Science,"
     17-18.

Stanek, Rose Marie. "Hopkins and Philosophy," 19-21.

746. Srinivasa Iyengar, K. R. Gerard Manley Hopkins: The Man and the Poet. Calcutta: Oxford University Press; 194 pp.

747. Murphy, L. D. in Sunday Hindu [Madras], August 1, p. 10.

748. Wagner, Robert D. Gerard Manley Hopkins: The "Terrible Sonnets" and Other Poems of Desolation. Unpublished M.A. thesis, Columbia University.

749. Warren, Austin. "Gerard Manley Hopkins," Rage For Order. Chicago: University of Chicago Press, pp. 52-65.

750. Watts, Janet Flowers. The Sonnets of Gerard Manley Hopkins. Unpublished honors thesis, University of Oregon.

751. Weyand, Norman, S.J. Correspondence in America, LXXIX, No. 26 (October 2), 608.
[Reply to Doyle, in America, September 18.]

752. Yoggerst, Sister Mary Hilary. Gerard Manley Hopkins as a Critic of Coventry Patmore. Unpublished M.A. thesis, Marquette University.

1949

753. Alonso, Dámaso. "Seis Poemas de Hopkins," Trivium [Monterrey, Mexico], I, No. 3 (January), 10-17.

754. Behn, Irene. "Gerard Manley Hopkins," Stimmen der Zeit [Fribourg], CXLV, No. 3 (December), 172-178.

755. Boyle, Robert R. "A Footnote on 'The Windhover,'" America, LXXXII, No. 5 (November 5), 129-130.

756. Brennan, Joseph Xavier. Gerard Manley
     Hopkins: A Critical Interpretation of
     his Poetry. Unpublished M.A. thesis,
     Brown University.
757. Clemen, Wolfgang. "Die Tagebücher des
     Gerard Manley Hopkins," Merkur
     [Stuttgart], III, No. 6 (January),
     571-584.
758. Delaney, Joan. "'The Blessed Virgin
     Compared to the Air We Breathe': An
     Interpretation," The Clarke College
     Labarum [Dubuque, Iowa], XLI, No. 3
     (Summer), 201-214.
759. Devlin, Christopher. "Time's Eunuch,"
     The Month, n. s., I, No. 5 (May), 303-
     312.
760. Doyle, Louis F., S.J. "In the Valley of
     the Shadow of Hopkins," The Catholic
     World, CLXIX (May), 102-108.
761. Foote, Timothy Gilson. To What Serves
     Mortal Agony? A Study of Hopkins'
     "The Wreck of the Deutschland" in
     Relation to "Lycidas," and an Analysis
     of the "Terrible Sonnets" in Relation
     to the Spiritual Exercises of St.
     Ignatius: the Whole Being Related
     Generally to Milton. Unpublished
     honors thesis, Harvard University.
762. [Foote, Timothy Gilson]. The Wreck of
     the Deutschland: An Elegy. Un-
     published Bowdoin Prize entry, Harvard
     University.
763. Fussell, Paul, Jr. "A Note on 'The Wind-
     hover,'" Modern Language Notes, LXIV,
     No. 4 (April), 271.
764. Gardner, W. H. Gerard Manley Hopkins
     (1844-1889): A Study of Poetic Idio-
     syncrasy in Relation to Poetic Tradi-
     tion. London: Martin Secker and
     Warburg, II; xiv, 415 pp.

765. Anon. in The Listener, XLII (July 14),
        77.
766. Anon. in The Times Literary Supplement
        (London), September 23, p. 616.
767. Conley, John. in Poetry, LXXIV, No. 5.
        (August), 292-300.
768. F[aussett], H. I'A[nson]. in The Man-
        chester Guardian, May 31, p. 4.
769. Grace, William J. in Books on Trial,
        VII, No. 7 (March), 258.
770. Grisewood, Harman. in The Tablet,
        August 13, p. 104.
771. Kennedy, Leo. in Chicago Sun Book Week,
        December 5, p. 53.
772. Nicholson, Norman. in The Fortnightly,
        n. s., No. 991 (July), pp. 65-66.
773. Peschmann, Hermann. in English, VII,
        No. 42 (Autumn), 295-296.
774. Peters, W. A. M. in The Month, n. s.,
        II, No. 4 (October), 269-273.
775. Pick, John. in The Catholic World, CLXX
        (December), 238-239.
776. Pick, John. in The Kenyon Review, XI,
        No. 1 (Winter), 155-159.
777. Price, R. G. G. in The English Review
        Magazine, III, No. 3 (September), 212.
778. Treneer, Anne. in Time & Tide, XXX, No.
        29 (July 16), 726-727.
[708]. Gardner, W. H. Poems of Gerard Manley
        Hopkins. 1948.
    [767]. Conley, John. in Poetry, LXXIV, No. 5
        (August), 292-300.
    779. Edridge, Ray. in The Downside Review,
        LXVII, No. 208 (April), 231-232.
    [769]. Grace, William J. in Books on Trial,
        VII, No. 7 (March), 258.
    780. Peschmann, Hermann. in English, VII, No.
        40 (Spring), 197-198.

[776]. Pick, John. in The Kenyon Review, XI,
        No. 1 (Winter), 155-159.
   781. Turner, Luke, O.P. in Blackfriars, XXX,
        No. 346 (January), 40.
782. Gardner, W. H. "The Religious Problem in
      G. M. Hopkins," in Critiques and Essays
      in Criticism: 1920-1948, ed. Robert
      Wooster Stallman. New York: The
      Ronald Press Company, pp. 346-357.
      [Reprinted from Scrutiny, 1937.]
783. Graves, Robert. The Common Asphodel:
      Collected Essays on Poetry, 1922-1949.
      London: Hamish Hamilton, pp. 99-101.
784. Hache, Mother Irene Marie, R.C.E. The
      Place of the Incarnation in the Poetry
      of Gerard Manley Hopkins. Unpublished
      M.A. thesis, Boston College.
785. Hass, Hans-Egon. "Gerard Manley Hopkins,"
      Begegnung [Cologne], IV, No. 7 (July),
      209-212.
786. Heuser, E. A. An Investigation of the
      Poetic Imagery of Gerard Manley Hopkins.
      Unpublished M.A. thesis, McGill Uni-
      versity.
[677]. Holloway, Sister Marcella Marie. The
       Prosodic Theory of Gerard Manley
       Hopkins. 1947.
   787. Shapiro, Karl. in Modern Language Notes,
         LXIV, No. 3 (March), 200-201.
788. House, Humphry. Correspondence in The
      Times Literary Supplement (London),
      November 4, p. 715.
      [Suggests the possibility of an
      acquaintanceship between Samuel Lucas
      (1818-1868) and Hopkins' father.]
789. Kahler, Erich. "Gerard Manley Hopkins:
      Gedichte," Merkur [Stuttgart], III,
      No. 6 (June), 565-570.

790. Kemp, Friedhelm. "Gerard Manley Hopkins,"
      Hochland [Munich], XLI, No. 4 (April),
      385-389.
791. Maltman, Sister M. Nicholas. The Odd
      Words in the Poetry of Gerard Manley
      Hopkins. Unpublished M.A. thesis, The
      Catholic University of America.
792. McDonough, Mary Lou. An Investigation to
      Determine the Extent of the Liturgical
      Echoes in the English Poems of Gerard
      Manley Hopkins. Unpublished M.A. thesis,
      Bowling Green State University.
793. Meyerstein, E. H. W. Correspondence in
      The Times Literary Supplement London ,
      November 11, p. 733.
      [On "The Loss of the Eurydice."]
794. Morgan, Edwin. Correspondence in The
      Times Literary Supplement (London),
      May 27, p. 347.
      [On "The Windhover."]
795. Nelson, Norman Kent. Gerard Manley
      Hopkins' Analysis and Interpretation
      of Three Representative Sonnets. Un-
      published M.A. thesis, Duke University.
796. Nicol, B. De Bear. Correspondence in The
      Times Literary Supplement (London),
      May 13, p. 313.
797. Orr, P. A. The Artistic Principles of
      Gerard Manley Hopkins. Unpublished
      M.A. thesis, McGill University.
798. Owen, B. Evan. "In Defence of Hopkins,"
      British Weekly [London], February 3,
      p. 4.
[721]. Peters, W. A. M., S.J. Gerard Manley
      Hopkins: A Critical Essay Towards
      the Understanding of his Poetry.
      1948.
   799. Bett, Henry. In British Weekly [London],
         January 13, p. 7.

800. Callahan, Virginia Woods. in <u>Books on</u>
     <u>Trial</u>, VII, No. 7 (March), 258.

[767]. Conley, John. in <u>Poetry</u>, LXXIV, No. 5
     (August), 292-300.

801. Deutsch, Babette. in <u>New York Herald</u>
     <u>Tribune Weekly Book Review</u>, January 2,
     p. 11.

802. Forster, Leonard. in <u>English Studies</u>
     [Amsterdam], XXX, No. 1 (February),
     18-20.

803. Lloyd Thomas, M.G. in <u>The Cambridge</u>
     <u>Journal</u>, II, No. 7 (April), 438-440.

[776]. Pick, John. in <u>The Kenyon Review</u>, XI,
     No. 1 (Winter), 155-159.

804. Pick, John. in <u>Thought</u>, XXIV, No. 94
     (September), 534-536.

805. Winters, Yvor. in <u>The Hudson Review</u>, II,
     No. 1 (Spring), 89-93.

806. Ricker, Elizabeth Ann. <u>The Relation of</u>
     <u>Hopkins' Theories of Poetry to his</u>
     <u>Applied Criticisms</u>. Unpublished M.A.
     thesis, Boston College.

807. R[itz], J.-G. "La Vierge Marie Comparée
     à l'air que Nous Respirons," <u>Vin</u>
     <u>Nouveau</u> [Lyon], 3rd ser., No. 13, pp. 13-16.

808. Rothenstein, Elizabeth. "The Pre-
     Raphaelites and Ourselves," <u>The Month</u>,
     n. s., I, No. 3 (March), 180-198.

809. Sansom, Clive. Correspondence in <u>The</u>
     <u>Times Literary Supplement</u> (London),
     May 20, p. 329.
     [Reply to Nicol, in <u>TLS</u>, May 13; on
     "The Windhover."]

810. Sargent, Daniel. "The Charm and the
     Strangeness: Gerard Manly [<u>sic</u>]
     Hopkins," <u>The Atlantic Monthly</u>, CLXXXIV,
     No. 2 (August), 73-77.

811.   Schneider, Elisabeth. "Hopkins' 'My Own
       Heart Let Me Have More Pity On,'" The
       Explicator, VII, No. 7 (May), item 49.
[746]. Srinivasa Iyengar, K. R. Gerard Manley
       Hopkins: The Man and the Poet.
       1948.
    812. Bewley, Marius. in Partisan Review, XVI,
          No. 5 (May), 543-547.
    [767]. Conley, John. in Poetry, LXXIV, No. 5,
          (August), 292-300.
    813. Gardner, W. H. in The Month, n. s., I,
          No 4 (April), 282-285.
    [776]. Pick, John. in The Kenyon Review, XI,
          No. 1 (Winter), 155-159.
    814. Pick John. in Renascence, I, No. 2
          (Spring), 57-58.
815.   Stobie, Margaret R. "Patmore's Theory
       and Hopkins' Practice," University of
       Toronto Quarterly, XIX, No. 1 (October),
       64-80.
816.   Symes, Gordon. "Hopkins, Herbert, and
       Contemporary Modes," The Hibbert
       Journal, XLVII, No. 4 (July), 389-394.
817.   Torchiana, Donald Thornhill. Pater,
       Newman, and the Poetic Development of
       G. M. Hopkins. Unpublished M.A. thesis,
       University of Iowa.
818.   Valette, Jacques. "Gerard Manley Hopkins,"
       Mercure de France, CCCVII (November 1).
       529-532.
819.   Weyand, Norman, ed. Immortal Diamond:
       Studies in Gerard Manley Hopkins.
       New York: Sheed & Ward; xxvi, 451 pp.
       Bonn, John Louis, S.J. "Greco-Roman
       Verse Theory and Gerard Manley Hopkins,"
       73-92.
       Boyle, Robert R., S.J. "The Thought
       Structure of 'The Wreck of the Deutsch-
       land,'" 333-350.

Burns, Chester A., S. J. "Gerard Manley
Hopkins, Poet of Ascetic and Aesthetic
Conflict." 175-191.
Carroll, Martin C., S.J. "Gerard Manley
Hopkins and the Society of Jesus," 3-
50.
MacGillivray, Arthur, S.J. "Hopkins and
Creative Writing," 51-72.
McNamee, Maurice B., S.J. "Hopkins, Poet
of Nature and of the Supernatural,"
222-251.
Noon, William T., S.J. "The Three Lan-
guages of Poetry," 252-274.
Ong, Walter J., S.J. "Hopkins' Sprung
Rhythm and the Life of English Poetry,"
93-174.
Schoder, Raymond V., S.J. "An Interpretive
Glossary of Difficult Words in the
'Poems,'" 192-221.
Schoder, Raymond V., S.J. "What Does
'The Windhover' Mean?" 275-306.
Watson, Youree, S.J. "'The Loss of the
Eurydice,' A Critical Analysis," 307-
332.
Weyand, Norman, S.J. "A Chronological
Hopkins Bibliography," 393-436.
Weyand, Norman, S.J. "Appendix: The
Historical Basis of 'The Wreck of the
Deutschland' and 'The Loss of the
Eurydice,'" 353-392.
820. Anon. in The New Yorker, XXV, No. 8
(April), 95.
[812]. Bewley, Marius. in Partisan Review, XVI,
No. 5 (May), 543-547.
821. Bischoff, Dolph Anthony, S.J. in America,
LXXXI, No. 2 (April 16), 86.
822. Brooks, Edna Belle. in The Clarke College
Labarum [Dubuque, Iowa], XLI, No. 3
(Summer), 277-278.

823. Chase, John W. in <u>The New York Times Book Review</u>, September 18, sec. 7, p. 12.
[767]. Conley, John. in <u>Poetry</u>, LXXIV, No. 5 (August), 292-300.
824. Demarest, Donald. in <u>The Catholic Worker</u>, XVI, No. 2 (June), 8.
825. Demarest, Donald. in <u>The Commonweal</u>, L, No. 3 (April 29), 74.
826. Devlin, Fr. Christopher, S.J. in <u>Catholic Herald</u> [London], December 2, p. 6.
827. Fitzpatrick, Rev. A. M., S.T.D. in <u>The Catholic Universe Bulletin</u> [Cleveland], April 15, p. 7.
828. Grady, Rev. Thomas J. in <u>The New World</u> [Chicago], LVII, No. 14 (April 8), 15.
829. Gribben, J. C. in <u>The Cincinnati Enquirer</u>, April 30, p. 6.
830. Grisewood, Harman. in <u>The Tablet</u>, December 3, pp. 380-381.
831. Halsband, Robert. in <u>The Saturday Review of Literature</u>, XXXIII, No. 18 (April 30), 12-13.
832. Laube, Clifford J. in <u>The Sign</u>, XXVIII, No. 10 (May), 59.
833. Nims, John Frederick. in <u>Chicago Sunday Tribune</u>, May 29, sec. 4, p. 6.
834. Rolfs, Alvin R. in <u>St. Louis Post-Dispatch</u>, April 15, sec. C , p. 2.
835. S., G. in <u>San Francisco Chronicle</u>, "This World" supplement, September 11, p. 23.
836. Scott, W. T. in <u>Providence Sunday Journal</u>, May 8, sec. VI, p. 10.
837. Shaw, J. G. in <u>The Ensign</u> [Ottawa, Canada], I, No. 29 (May 14), 10.
838. Shuster, George N. in <u>New York Herald Tribune Weekly Book Review</u>, April 17, sec. 7, p. 7.

839. Wright, Cecelia. in The Catholic Alumnae
     Quarterly, XXXII, No. 4 (December), 39.
840. Winters, Yvor. "The Poetry of Gerard
     Manley Hopkins," The Hudson Review, I,
     No. 4 (Winter), 455-476; II, No. 1
     (Spring), 61-89.

1950

841. Akey, John. Liturgical Imagery in the
     Poetry of Gerard Manley Hopkins,
     Thomas Merton, and Robert Lowell. Un-
     published M.A. thesis, University of
     Vermont.
842. Baker, James V. "The Lark in English
     Poetry," Prairie Schooner, XXIV, No. 1
     (Spring), 70-79.
843. Baron, Ronald. "Traduciendo a Hopkins,"
     Criterio [Buenos Aires], XXIII
     (December 21), 1005-1010.
844. Blum, Sister Magdalen Louise, S.C. The
     Imagery in the Poetry of Gerard Manley
     Hopkins. Unpublished M.A. thesis,
     University of New Mexico.
845. Brophy, James D., Jr. The Early Poems of
     Gerard Manley Hopkins and their Place
     in Hopkins Criticism. Unpublished
     M.A. thesis, Columbia University.
846. Charney, Maurice. "A Bibliographical
     Study of Hopkins Criticism: 1918-1949."
     Thought, XXV, No. 97 (June), 297-326.
847. Cohen, Selma Jean. "Hopkins' 'As King-
     fishers Catch Fire,'" Modern Language
     Quarterly, XI, No. 2 (June), 197-204.
848. Coogan, Marjorie D. "Inscape and Instress:
     Further Analogies with Scotus,"
     Publications of the Modern Language
     Association of America, LXV, No. 2
     (March), 66-74.

849.   Corr, Gerard M., O.S.M. "Our Lady's
       Praise in Gerard Manley Hopkins," The
       Clergy Review, n. s., XXXIII, No. 5
       (May), 289-294.
850.   Devlin, Christopher. "The Image and the
       Word," The Month, n. s., III, No. 2
       (February), 114-127; No. 3 (March),
       191-202.
851.   Devlin, Christopher. Correspondence in
       The Month, n. s., IV, No. 3 (Septem-
       ber), 213-215.
       [Reply to Gardner, in The Month, Sep-
       tember.]
852.   Freeman, Beatrice D. The Literary Repu-
       tation of Gerard Manley Hopkins. Un-
       published M.A. thesis, Columbia Uni-
       versity.
853.   Gardner, W. H. Correspondence in The
       Month, n. s., IV, No. 3 (September),
       210-213.
       [Reply to Devlin, in The Month,
       February and March.]
[764]. Gardner, W. H. GMH: A Study of Poetic
       Idiosyncrasy in Relation to Poetic
       Tradition. II. 1949.
       854.   Anon. in The New Yorker, XXV, No. 52
              (February 18), 90-91.
       855.   Every, George, S.S.M. in Poetry [London],
              V, No. 18 (May), 22-24.
       856.   La Drière, Craig. in The Journal of
              Aesthetics & Art Criticism, IX, No. 2
              (December), 153-154.
       857.   Miles, Josephine. in The Yale Review,
              XXXIX, No. 2 (Winter), 368-370.
       858.   Pick, John. in The Thomist, XIII, No. 2
              (April), 289-296.
       859.   Tyne, James L. in Thought, XXV, No. 97
              (June), 352-353.

[708]. Gardner, W. H. Poems of Gerard Manley
        Hopkins. 1948.
    [856]. La Drière, Craig. in The Journal of
        Aesthetics & Art Criticism, IX, No. 2
        (December), 153-154.
860. Gormon, Patrick. The Attitude to Nature
     and the External World of Gerard
     Manley Hopkins. Unpublished M.A.
     thesis, University of Toronto.
861. Griffin, Sister Mary Ignatia. Gerard
     Manley Hopkins' "That Nature is a
     Heraclitean Fire and Of the Comfort of
     the Resurrection": An Analysis of
     Meaning. Unpublished M.A. thesis, The
     Catholic University of America.
862. Gutiérrez Mora, José Manuel. "Dos Poetas
     Ingleses (Tennyson y Hopkins)," Et
     Caetera [Guadalajara], I, No. 2 (April-
     June), supplement, pp. 1-15.
863. Heilsam, Ingeborg. Die Oxfordbewegung
     und ihr Einfluss auf die Englische
     Dichtung: Hopkins, Patmore, Thompson,
     Newman. Unpublished Ph.D. dissertation,
     University of Vienna.
864. Hoecker, Eric L. Hopkins, Joyce, and the
     Development of the Artist. Unpublished
     M.A. thesis, Columbia University.
865. Howarth. R. G. "Hopkins and Sir Thomas
     More," Notes and Queries, CXCV, No.
     20 (September 30), 438.
[622]. The Kenyon Critics. Gerard Manley
        Hopkins. 1945.
    866. Anon. in The Listener, XLIII (April 13),
         664.
    867. Devlin, Christopher, S.J. in The Month,
         n. s., IV, No. 2 (August), 141.
868. Lees, F. N. "'The Windhover,'" Scrutiny,
     XVII, No. 1 (Spring), 32-37.

869. Mullany, Stephen William. Religious
      Elements in Hopkins' Poetry. Un-
      published M.A. thesis, University of
      Iowa.
870. Owen, B. Evan. "Gerard Manley Hopkins,"
      The Fortnightly Review, n. s., CLXVIII
      (July), 38-42.
871. Patricia, Sister Mary, C.S.J. "Forty
      Years of Criticism: A Chronological
      Check List of Criticism of the Works
      of Gerard Manley Hopkins from 1909 to
      1949," Bulletin of Bibliography, XX,
      No. 2 (May-August), 38-44; No. 3
      (September-December), 63-67.
[721]. Peters, W. A. M., S.J. GMH: A Critical
      Essay Towards the Understanding of
      his Poetry. 1948.
      [856]. La Drière, Craig. in The Journal of
              Aesthetics & Art Criticism, IX, No.
              2 (December), 153-154.
      [858]. Pick, John. in The Thomist, XIII, No.
              2 (April), 289-296.
872. Robson, W. W. Correspondence in The
      Times Literary Supplement (London),
      February 24, p. 121.
      [On Hopkins and Congreve; an image in
      "The Windhover" from The Way of the
      World.]
[687]. Ruggles, Eleanor. Gerard Manley
      Hopkins: A Life. 1947.
      873. Guidi, Augusto. in Rivista di Letteratura
            Moderne [Florence], I, No. 1 (July),
            71.
874. Scanlan, Sister Alissa Marie. A Study of
      Gerard Manley Hopkins' Dramatic Frag-
      ment, "St. Winefred's Well." Un-
      published M.A. thesis, The Catholic
      University of America.

875. Schneider, Elisabeth. "Two Metaphysical
      Images in Hopkins's 'The Wreck of the
      Deutschland,'" Modern Language Notes,
      LXV, No. 5 (May), 306-311.
876. Treneer, Anne. "The Criticism of Gerard
      Manley Hopkins," in The Penguin New
      Writing, No. 40, ed. John Lehmann.
      Harmondsworth, Middlesex: Penguin
      Books Ltd., pp. 98-115.
877. Westerlinck, Albert. "Een Onsterfelijke
      Diamant: G. M. Hopkins," Dietsche
      Warande en Belfort [Amsterdam], No. 7
      (August-September), pp. 421-426.
[819]. Weyand, Norman, ed. Immortal Diamond:
        Studies in GMH.   1949.
      878. Anon. in The Listener, XLIII (March 9),
            443-444.
      879. Anon. in The Standard [Dublin], January
            27, p. 3.
      880. Clark, Eleanor Grace. in The Catholic
            World, CLXXI (April), 78-79.
      881. Gardner, W. H. in The Month, n. s., III,
            No. 3 (March), 217-221.
      882. Gleeson, W. in Thought, XXV, No. 98
            (September), 528-530.
      883. Haynes, Renee. in Time & Tide, XXXI, No.
            10 (March 11), 234.
      884. Heppenstall, Rayner. in The New States-
            man and Nation, n. s., XXXIX, No. 995
            (April 1), 377-378.
      [856]. La Drière, Craig. in The Journal of
              Aesthetics & Art Criticism, IX, No.
              2 (December), 153-154.
      [858]. Pick, John. in The Thomist, XIII, No.
              2 (April), 289-296.
      885. Routh, H. V. in The Adelphi, n. s.,
            XXVI, No. 2, 210-211.
      886. Spender, Stephen. in Universities
            Quarterly, IV, No. 3 (May), 293-295.

887. Woodring. Carl R. "Once More 'The Wind-
      hover,'" The Western Review, XV, No. 1
      (Autumn), 61-64.

                    1951
888. Auden, W. H. "A Knight of the Infinite,"
      in Literary Opinion in America, ed. M.
      D. Zabel. Rev. ed. New York: Harper
      & Brothers, pp. 253-255.
      [Reprinted from The New Republic,
      August, 1944.]
889. Bailey, Joseph G. The Sonnet Theory of
      Gerard Manley Hopkins. Unpublished
      M.A. thesis, The Catholic University of
      America.
890. Bischoff, D. Anthony, S.J. "The Manu-
      scripts of Gerard Manley Hopkins,"
      Thought, XXVI, No. 103 (Winter), 551-
      580.
891. Cohen, J. M. "The Road Not Taken: A
      Study in the Poetry of Robert Bridges,"
      The Cambridge Journal, IV, No. 9
      (June), 555-564.
892. Davie, Donald A. "Hopkins, The Decadent
      Critic," The Cambridge Journal, IV,
      No. 12 (September), 725-739.
893. Dever, Joe. "Poet of Beauty," Today
      [National Catholic Magazine, Chicago],
      VI, No. 5 (February), 18.
894. Digges, Sister Mary Laurentia. Gerard
      Manley Hopkins' Sonnets of Desolation:
      An Analysis of Meaning. Washington,
      D. C.: The Catholic University of America
      Press; xi, 156 pp.
895. Ellrodt, R. "Grandeur et Misère de
      Gérard Manley Hopkins," Cahiers du Sud
      [Marseilles], XXXIII, No. 306, 272-289.

896. Garvey, Mother Eugenia Marie, O.S.U.
     Gerard Manley Hopkins, S.J.: His
     Criticism of the Major Writers in
     English Literature. Unpublished M.A.
     thesis, Fordham University.
897. Gwynn, Frederick L. "Hopkins' 'The Wind-
     hover': A New Simplification," Modern
     Language Notes, LXVI, No. 6 (June),
     366-370.
898. Mlodzik, Sister Mary Nazaria, O.P. A
     Study of the Parallelism and Evolution
     in the Imagery of Gerard Manley Hopkins.
     Unpublished M.A. thesis, University of
     Detroit.
899. Patmore, Derek. "Three Poets Discuss New
     Verse Forms," The Month, n. s., VI,
     No. 2 (August), 69-78.
900. Pearson, W. H. "G. M. Hopkins and Provost
     Fortescue," Notes and Queries, CXCVI,
     No. 20 (September), 431-433.
901. Pinto, Vivian de Sola. "Hopkins and
     Bridges," Crisis in English Poetry:
     1880-1940. London: Hutchinson Uni-
     versity Library, pp. 59-84.
902. Raymond, William O. "'The Mind's Internal
     Heaven' in Poetry," University of
     Toronto Quarterly, XX, No. 3 (April),
     215-232.
903. Reeves, James. "The Study of Poetry:
     with Notes on Gerard Manley Hopkins,"
     Use of English, II, No. 3 (Spring),
     130-136.
904. Retinger, Sister Mary Anthony. Gerard
     Manley Hopkins as a Critic of English
     Literature. Unpublished M.A. thesis,
     DePaul University.
905. Robinson, Brian L. Nature in the Poetry
     of Gerard Manley Hopkins. Unpublished
     M.A. thesis, Columbia University.

[819]. Weyand, Norman, ed. Immortal Diamond:
          Studies in GMH. 1949.
          906. Lloyd Thomas, M. G. in The Review of
                English Studies, n. s., II, No. 8
                (October), 397-399.
907. Wright, Brooks. "Hopkins' 'God's Gran-
      deur,'" The Explicator, X, No. 1
      (October), item 5.
908. Ziemba, Walter J. Gerard Manley Hopkins'
      "Tom's Garland: Upon the Unemployed":
      An Analysis. Unpublished M.A. thesis, The
      Catholic University of America.

                    1952
909. Begley, J. E. The Literary Criticisms
      of Gerard Manley Hopkins. Unpublished
      M.A. thesis, University of Melbourne.
910. Bischoff, Dolph Anthony. Gerard Manley
      Hopkins as Literary Critic. Un-
      published Ph.D. dissertation, Yale
      University.
911. Campbell, Roy. "Inscape of Skytehawks on
      the Cookhouse Roof (In Homage to
      Gerard Manley Hopkins)," Nine, III,
      No. 3 (April), 272.
      [Poem.]
912. [Carroll, Patrick J., C.S.C.]. Editorial
      in The Ave Maria, LXXV, No. 19 (May
      10), 582.
      [Reply to Ward, in The Month, July.]
913. Charboneau, Reverend Damian M., O.S.M.
      "Hopkins: Poet Laureate of Mary and
      May," The Magnificat, XC, No. 1 (May),
      5-7.
914. Durr, Robert A. "Hopkins' 'No Worst,
      There Is None,'" The Explicator, XI,
      No. 2 (November), item 11.

915. Futrell, John Carroll, S.J.   "Gerard
     Manley Hopkins and God's 'Poem of
     Beauty,'" The Catholic World, CLXXIV
     (February), 352-358.
916. Gardner, Ralph. "Two Jesuits," The Mod-
     ern Churchman, XLII, No. 4 (December),
     350-359.
917. Gardner, W. H. "The Achievement of
     Coventry Patmore," The Month, n. s.,
     VII, No. 2 (February, 89-98; No. 4
     (April), 220-230.
918. Gleeson, William F., Jr. Gerard Manley
     Hopkins and the Society of Jesus.
     Unpublished M.A. thesis, Columbia
     University.
919. Guidi, Augusto. Poesie di Gerard Manley
     Hopkins: con testo a fronte Traduzione
     Intraduzione e Note. (Collana Fenice,
     No. 10.) Parma: Gudanda; 260 pp.
920. Gutiérrez Mora, Jose Manuel. "Diez
     Sonetos de Hopkins," Ábside [Mexico
     City], XVI, No. 3 (July-September),
     305-320.
921. Hansen-Löve, Friedrich. "Der Dichter der
     Schöpfung: Ein Hinweis auf Gerard
     Manley Hopkins," Wort und Wahrheit
     [Vienna], VII, No. 6 (June), 457-460.
922. Hart, Sister Mary Adorita. The Christo-
     centric Theme in Gerard Manley Hopkins'
     "The Wreck of the Deutschland,"
     Washington, D. C." The Catholic University
     of America Press; viii, 178 pp.
923. Healy, Sister M. Aquinas, R.S.M. "Milton
     and Hopkins," University of Toronto
     Quarterly, XXII, No. 1 (October), 18-
     25.
924. Jeremy, Sr. Mary. "Hopkins and St.
     Gertrude," The Times Literary Supple-
     ment (London), November 14, p. 743.

925. Keane, James F. An Analysis of Gerard
      Manley Hopkins' Sonnet, "Henry Purcell."
      Unpublished M.A. thesis, The Catholic
      University of America.
926. Leavis, F. R. "Gerard Manley Hopkins"
      and "The Letters of Gerard Manley
      Hopkins," The Common Pursuit. New
      York: George W. Stewart, Inc., pp. 44-
      58 and 58-72.
927. Lynch, John W. "Gerard Manley Hopkins,"
      Hourglass: Stories of a Measured Year.
      New York: The Macmillan Company, pp.
      151-153.
928. McCarthy, Adrian James. The Concept of
      Inscape in the Poetry of Gerard Manley
      Hopkins. Unpublished M.A. thesis,
      New York University.
929. McCormick, Sister Mary James, O.P.
      Gerard Manley Hopkins' "Spelt from
      Sibyl's Leaves": An Analysis. Un-
      published M.A. thesis, The Catholic Uni-
      versity of America.
930. McDonald, Sister Mary Roy. Gerard Manley
      Hopkins as Social Critic. Unpublished
      M.A. thesis, Marquette University.
931. Mercer, W. C. "G. M. Hopkins and Richard
      Jefferies," Notes and Queries, CXCVII,
      No. 10 (May), 217.
932. Meuth, Georgeanna S. Gerard Manley
      Hopkins: Creator and Created. Un-
      published M.A. thesis, Columbia
      University.
933. Micklewright, F. H. Amphlett. "G. M.
      Hopkins and Provost Fortescue," Notes
      and Queries, CXCVII, No. 8 (April 12),
      169-172, 174; No. 17 (August 16), 365-
      366.

934. Pearson, W. H. A Comparative Study of
      Patmore, Hopkins, and Francis Thompson,
      Entailing an Examination of Their
      Leading Ideas and Their Poetic Tech-
      niques. Unpublished Ph.D. dissertation,
      University of London.
935. Pitchford, Lois W. "The Curtal Sonnets
      of Gerard Manley Hopkins," Modern
      Language Notes, LXVII, No. 3 (March),
      165-169.
936. Sharp, Jean Margaret. A Cycle of Nine
      Songs for Soprano to Poems of Gerard
      Manley Hopkins. Unpublished M.A.
      thesis, University of Washington.
937. Taylor, E. K. "Gerard Manley Hopkins:
      A Poet for Priests," The Clergy Re-
      view, n. s., XXXVII, No. 7 (July),
      394-404.
938. Ward, Dennis. "Gerard Manley Hopkins's
      'Spelt from Sibyl's Leaves,'" The
      Month, n. s., VIII, No. 1 (July), 40-
      51.
939. Wilder, Amos N. Modern Poetry and the
      Christian Tradition: A Study in the
      Relation of Christianity to Culture.
      New York: Charles Scribner's Sons,
      pp. 148-175, et passim.
940. Wolking, Sister Mary Theresa, O.S.B.
      Hopkins' "The Blessed Virgin Compared
      to the Air We Breathe": A Study in
      Unity. Unpublished M.A. thesis, The
      Catholic University of America.

                    1953
941. Anon. "The Axe and the Stone: A Note
      on Poetry and Criticism," Blue Guitar,
      I, No. 4 (April), unpaginated.

942. Anon. "Purchase of Manuscripts of Gerard
      Manley Hopkins," The Bodleian Library
      Record, IV, No. 6 (December), 290.
943. Charboneau, Rev. Damian M., O.S.M.
      "Gerald [sic] Manley Hopkins: Poet
      Laureate of Mary and May," Our Lady's
      Digest, VIII, No. 1 (May), 40-43.
      [Condensed from Magnificat, May, 1952.]
944. Coombes, H[enry]. Literature and
      Criticism. London: Chatto & Windus,
      pp. 145-147, 156-159, et passim.
945. Crehan, J. H. "More Light on Gerard
      Hopkins," The Month, n. s., X, No. 4
      (October), 205-214.
946. Day Lewis, C. "Some Influences on Modern
      Poetry," The Listener, XLIX (January
      29), 185-187.
947. De Grunne, Dominique. "Technique du
      Poète: Gerard Manley Hopkins,"
      Critique [Paris], IX, No. 74 (July),
      579-500.
948, Des Rochers, Sister Vitalis. Gerard
      Manley Hopkins; "As Kingfishers Catch
      Fire, Dragonflies Draw Flame": A
      Study in Artistic Unity. Unpublished
      M.A. thesis, The Catholic University of
      America.
949. Gardner, W. H. "Introduction," Poems
      and Prose of Gerard Manley Hopkins.
      Harmondsworth, Middlesex: Penguin
      Books Ltd., pp. xiii-xxxvii.
   950. Anon. in The Times Literary Supplement
        (London), November 13, p. 730.
   951. Fraser, G. S. in The New Statesman and
        Nation, n. s., XLVI (October 10), 424-
        425.

952. Gerken, John Diedrich, S.J. The Date and
     Sequence of the Terrible Sonnets of
     Gerard M. Hopkins, S.J. Unpublished
     M.A. thesis, Loyola University
     [Chicago].
953. Gross, Robert Eugene. The Criticism of
     Gerard Manley Hopkins' "The Windhover,"
     Unpublished M.A. thesis, New York
     University.
954. Heuser, Edward Alan. The Development of
     Aesthetic Cognition in Gerard Manley
     Hopkins. Unpublished Ph.D. disser-
     tation, Harvard University.
955. McGaughran, Sister Ruth Marie, S.C.N. The
     Poetry of Gerard Manley Hopkins Em-
     bodies Traditional Aesthetics. Un-
     published M.A. thesis, Xavier University.
956. MacNeil, Stella Therese. The Poetry of
     Thos. Merton Considered in Relation to
     that of Gerard Manley Hopkins. Un-
     published M.A. thesis, New York Uni-
     versity.
957. Marcotte, John Paul. A Philosophical
     Presentation of the Aesthetic-Poetics
     of Gerard Manley Hopkins as Inferred
     from Scape and Inscape, with its
     Significance as a New Critique. Un-
     published M.A. thesis, Saint John's
     University.
958. Melchiori, Giorgio. "Due Manieristi:
     Henry James e G. M. Hopkins," Lo
     Spettatore Italino [Rome], VI, No. 1
     (January), 20-27.
959. Morris, David. The Poetry of Gerard
     Manley Hopkins and T. S. Eliot in the
     Light of the Donne Tradition: A
     Comparative Study. (Swiss Studies in
     English, No. 33) Berne: A. Francke;
     144 pp.

960. Pick, John. "Introduction," A Hopkins
      Reader. London and New York: Oxford
      University Press, pp. xi-xxvii.
      961. Anon. in The Nation, CLXXIV, No. 23
            (June 6), 486.
      962. Anon. in The New Yorker, XXIX, No. 30
            (September 12), 135-136.
      963. Anon. in Notes and Queries, n. s., I,
            No. 9 (September), 411-412.
      964. Anon. in Time, LXI, No. 21 (May 25), 106.
      965. Anon. in The Times Literary Supplement
            (London), June 5, p. 366.
      966. Ames, Ruth M. in The Catholic World,
            CLXXVII (August), 397-398.
      967. F[aussett], H. I'A[nson]. in The Man-
            chester Guardian, June 16, p. 4.
      [951]. Fraser, G. S. in The New Statesman
              and Nation, n. s., XLVI (October
              10), 424-425.
      968. Gardner, W. H. in The Month, n. s., X,
            No. 5 (November), 304-308.
      969. Gillet, Eric. in The National and English
            Review, CXLI, No. 845 (July), 50.
      970. Grady, Rev. Thomas J. in Books on Trial,
            XI, No. 8 (June), 333.
      971. Gregory, Horace. in The New York Times
            Book Review, August 2, p. 5.
      972. H[alsband],R[obert]. in The Saturday Re-
            view, XXXVI, No. 31 (August 1), 13.
      973. Hasley, Louis. in The Ave Maria, LXXVIII,
            No. 19 (November 7), 24.
      974. Hasley, Louis. in Today, IX, No. 1
            (October), 21.
      975. McDonald, Gerald D. in Library Journal,
            LXXVIII, No. 14 (August), 1334.
      976. McLuhan, Marshall. in The Commonweal,
            LVIII, No. 13 (July 3), 326-327.
      977. Meath, Gerard, O.P. in Blackfriars,
            XXXIV, No. 402 (September), 413-415.

978. Moloney, Michael F. in America, LXXXIX,
     No. 23 (September 5), 555-557.
979. Peschmann, Hermann. in English, IX, No.
     54 (Autumn), 224-225.
980. Reeves, James. in The Listener, XLIX
     (June 25), 1060-1063.
981. Richardson, Joanna. in The Spectator,
     CXCI, (August 28), 226.
982. Schoder, Raymond V. in Thought, XXVIII,
     No. 111 (Winter), 619-621.
983. Slevin, Gerard. in The Tablet, CCII
     (August 8), 133-134.
984. Speaight, Robert. in The Dublin Review,
     CXXVII, No. 462 (Winter), 371-380.
985. Stauffer, Robert E. in Voices, No. 152
     (September-October), pp. 55-57.
986. Steuert, Dom Hilary. in The Downside Re-
     view, LXXI, No. 226 (Autumn), 459-461.
987. Thornton, Francis Beauchesne. in
     Catholic Digest, XVIII, No. 1.
     (November), 105-106.
988. Veetch, T. in The Australasian Catholic
     Record [Sydney], XXX, No. 4 (October),
     335-338.
989. Read, Herbert Edward. The True Voice of
     Feeling, Studies in English Romantic
     Poetry. London: Faber and Faber, pp.
     76-86.
990. Reeves, James. "Introduction: The Man
     and the Poems," Selected Poems of
     Gerard Manley Hopkins. London:
     Heinemann Educational Books Ltd., pp.
     viii-xxviii.
     [965]. Anon. in The Times Literary Supplement
            (London), June 5, p. 366.
     [968]. Gardner, W. H. in The Month, n. s., X,
            No. 5 (November), 304-308.
     [977]. Meath, Gerard, O.P. in Blackfriars,
            XXXIV, No. 402 (September), 413-415.

[979]. Peschmann, Hermann. in English, IX,
        No. 54 (Autumn), 224-225.
[981]. Richardson, Joanna. in The Spectator,
        CXCI (August 28), 226.
[983]. Slevin, Gerard. in The Tablet, CCII
        (August 8), 133-134.
[984]. Speaight, Robert. in The Dublin Review,
        CXXVII, No. 462 (Winter), 371-380.
991. Sehrt, Ernst Th. "Gerard Manly [sic]
        Hopkins: Eine deutsche Ausgabe," Die
        Sammlung [Göttingen], X, No. 4 (April),
        215-219.

1954

992. Abbott, C. Colleer. Correspondence in
        The Times Literary Supplement (London),
        October 29, p. 696.
        [Note on Hopkins' letters.]
993. Clemen, W. and U. Gerard Manley Hopkins:
        Gedichte, Schriften, Briefe. Munich:
        Kösel-Verlag; 744 pp.
994. Clines, Gerald Patrick. Gerard Manley
        Hopkins' Ascetic-Aesthetic Conflict.
        Unpublished senior thesis, University
        of Santa Clara.
995. Connellan, Sister Anne Miriam, S.C. An
        Analysis of the Qualitative Structure
        of Sound in "The Wreck of the Deutsch-
        land" by Gerard Manley Hopkins. Un-
        published M.A. thesis, The Catholic Uni-
        versity of America.
996. Consolata, Sister Mary. "A Theme Song
        for the Marian Year," America, XC, No.
        19 (February 6), 480-482.
        [On "The Blessed Virgin Compared to the
        Air We Breathe."]
997. Couldrey, Oswald. Correspondence in The
        Times Literary Supplement (London),
        September 24, p. 609.
        [On "The Windhover."]

998.   Curran, John Patrick. "Inscape" and "In-
       stress" as Related Principles in the
       Theory and Practice of Gerard Manley
       Hopkins. Unpublished M.A. thesis,
       New York University.
999.   D'Arcy, M. C. "A Note on Gerard Hopkins,"
       The Month, n. s., XI, No. 2 (February),
       113-115.
1000. Empson, W. Correspondence in The Times
       Literary Supplement (London), October
       1, p. 625.
       [On "The Windhover."]
1001. Empson, William. Correspondence in The
       Times Literary Supplement (London),
       October 29, p. 689.
       [Reply to Lees, in TLS, October 22;
       on "The Windhover."]
1002. Fitzgerald, Robert. "Generations of
       Leaves: The Poet in the Classical
       Tradition," Perspectives USA, No. 8
       (Summer), pp. 68-85.
1003. Fleming, Lenore Marie Moe. The In-
       fluence of Duns Scotus on Gerard
       Manley Hopkins. Unpublished M.A.
       thesis, Loyola University [Chicago].
[949]. Gardner, W. H. Poems and Prose of GMH.
       1953.
       1004. Ritz, J. G. in Etudes Anglaises, VII, No.
              3 (July), 342-343.
1005. Gerlach, Erika. "Gerard M. Hopkins,
       S.J.," Weltstimmen [Stuttgart], XXIII,
       No. 6 (June), 271-276.
1006. Goldhurst, Richard. "Translation: Sine
       qua non: Bowra and Hopkins," The
       Classical Journal, L, No. 1 (October),
       5-11.
1007. Gutiérrez Mora, José Manuel. Hopkinsiana:
       la vida, la obra y la supervivencia de
       Gerard Manley Hopkins. Mexico City:
       Aldina; 239 pp.

1008. Anon. in The Times Literary Supplement
        (London), August 13, pp. 509-510.
1009. Hartman, Geoffrey H. The Unmediated
        Vision: An Interpretation of Words-
        worth, Hopkins, Rilke, and Valéry.
        New Haven: Yale University Press,
        pp. 47-67, et passim.
1010. Lees, F. N. Correspondence in The Times
        Literary Supplement (London), September
        3, p. 557.
        [On "The Windhover."]
1011. Lees, F. N. Correspondence in The Times
        Literary Supplement (London), October
        22, p. 673.
        [Reply to Couldrey, in TLS, September
        24; on "The Windhover."]
1012. McBrien, William Augustine. Musical
        Techniques in the Versification of
        Gerard Manley Hopkins. Unpublished
        M.A. thesis, Saint John's University.
1013. Mambrino, J., S.J. "La Sainte Vierge
        comparée à l'air que Nous Respirons,"
        Christus [Paris], I, No. 3 (July),
        7-15.
1014. Martz, Louis L. The Poetry of Meditation:
        A Study in English Religious Litera-
        ture of the Seventeenth Century. New
        Haven: Yale University Press, pp.
        322-327, et passim.
1015. [Patterson], Jean Kenny. The Influence
        of Welsh Alliteration upon the Poetry
        of Gerard Manley Hopkins. Unpublished
        M.A. thesis, Fordham University.
1016. Peach, William W. Gerard Manley Hopkins:
        His Outlook on External Reality as it
        is Revealed in His Works. Unpublished
        senior thesis, University of Santa
        Clara.

1017. Peters, W. A. M., S.J. Correspondence
       in The Times Literary Supplement
       (London), October 29, p. 689.
       [On "The Windhover."]
[960]. Pick, John. A Hopkins Reader. 1953.
       1018. Anon. in Notes and Queries, n. s., I,
              No. 9 (September), 411-412.
       1019. Bradbrook, M. C. in The Modern Language
              Review, XLIX, No. 3 (July), 370.
       1020. McLuhan, Marshall. in Queen's Quarterly,
              LXI, No. 2 (Summer), 268-270.
       [1004]. Ritz, J. G. in Etudes Anglaises, VII,
              No. 3 (July), 342-343.
1021. Pick, John. "Hopkins' Imagery: The
       Relation of His Journal to His Poetry,"
       Renascence, VII, No. 1 (Autumn), 30-
       38.
1022. Templeman, William Darby. "Hopkins and
       Whitman: Evidences of Influence and
       Echoes," Philological Quarterly,
       XXXIII, No. 1 (January), 48-65.
1023. Turner, Brother H. Paul, F.S.C. An
       Indexed Synthesis of the Critical
       Thought of Gerard Manley Hopkins.
       Unpublished M.A. thesis, DePaul
       University.
1024. Wickham, John F. "Mariology in G.M.
       Hopkins," The Month, n. s., XII, No.
       3 (September), 161-172.

                        1955
1025. Abbott, Claude Colleer. "Introduction,"
       The Correspondence of Gerard Manley
       Hopkins and Richard Watson Dixon.
       Second impression. London: Oxford
       University Press, pp. xiii-xxxi.
                        and

1026. Abbott, Claude Colleer. "Introduction,"
The Letters of Gerard Manley Hopkins
to Robert Bridges. Second impression.
London: Oxford University Press, pp.
xv-xlvii.

1027. Anon. in America, XCIII, No. 21
(August 20), 496.

1028. O'Gorman, Ned. in The Commonweal, LXII,
No. 16 (July 22), 403-404.

1029. Adorita, Sister Mary, B.V.M. "Hopkins's
'wings that spell' in 'The Wreck of
the Deutschland,'" Modern Language
Notes, LXX, No. 5 (May), 345-347.

1030. Anderson, Walter J. "The Golden Echo":
Religion in the Life and Poetry of
Gerard Manley Hopkins (1844-1889).
Unpublished M.A. thesis, Trinity
College.

1031. Anon. "Difficulty Poetry," The Times
Literary Supplement (London), June
24, p. 349.
[On "The Windhover."]

1032. Bischoff, Anthony, S.J. "Hopkins,"
Jubilee, III, No. 1 (May), 20-29.

1033. Bogan, Louise. "The Letters of Gerard
Manley Hopkins," Selected Criticism,
Prose, Poetry. New York: The Noon-
day Press, pp. 42-47.
[Reprinted from The Nation, 1938.]

1034. Bowen, Robert O. "Hopkins and Welsh
Prosody," Renascence, VIII, No. 2
(Winter), 71-74, 87.

1035. Boyle, Robert Richard, S.J. The Nature
and Function of the Mature Imagery
of Gerard Manley Hopkins. Unpublished
Ph.D. dissertation, Yale University.

1036. Burgan, Sister Mary Stella Maris, S.S.
       N.D. A Study of Gerard Manley Hop-
       kins' Sonnet, "Andromeda," Un-
       published M.A. thesis, The Catholic Uni-
       versity of America.
1037. Byrne, Sister Mary Jean Catherine, O.P.
       A Synthesis of the Interpretations
       of "The Windhover." Unpublished M.A.
       thesis, The Catholic University of America.
1038. Cassidy, Lawrence P. Gerard Manley
       Hopkins' Ideas on Beauty and Truth as
       Shown in his Poems and Letters. Un-
       published M.A. thesis, DePaul Uni-
       versity.
[993]. Clemen, W. and U. Gerard Manley Hopkins:
       Gedichte. 1954.
       1039. Stenzel, H., S.J. in Stimmen der Zeit
              [Fribourg], CLVII, No. 3 (December),
              233.
1040. Cole, David Bruce. Charged with the
       Grandeur of God: God's Majesty, as
       Expressed in the Poetry of Gerard
       Manley Hopkins. Unpublished honors
       thesis, Harvard University.
1041. Cunningham, Maureen Michalla. The Poetry
       of Gerard Manley Hopkins, S.J.
       Unpublished M.A. thesis, University
       of Washington.
1042. Donoghue, Denis. "The Bird as Symbol:
       Hopkins's Windhover," Studies, XLIV,
       No. 175 (Autumn), 291-299.
1043. Donoghue, Denis. "Technique in Hopkins,"
       Studies, XLIV, No. 176 (Winter),
       446-456.
1044. Downes, David Anthony. The Ignatian
       Spirit in Gerard Manley Hopkins. Un-
       published Ph.D. dissertation, Univer-
       sity of Washington.
       [In Dissertation Abstracts, XVI, No.
       3 (February, 1956),535.]

1045. Eisenbraun, Meredith V. A Study of
       Gerard Manley Hopkins' Sonnets with
       Reference to His Own Commentary and
       to the Formative Influences in His
       Life. Unpublished M.A. thesis, Uni-
       versity of South Dakota.
1046. Empson, W. Correspondence in The Times
       Literary Supplement (London), May 20,
       p. 269.
       [On "The Windhover"; reply to Ritz,
       in TLS, May 6.]
1047. Faget, Sister Mary Ignatius. The Con-
       cept of Sake in Gerard Manley Hopkins.
       Unpublished M.A. thesis, The Catholic
       University of America.
1048. Gardner, W. H. Correspondence in The
       Times Literary Supplement (London),
       June 24, p. 349.
       [On "The Windhover"; reply to Ritz,
       in TLS, May 6.]
1049. Gerlach, Erika. "Gerard Manley Hopkins:
       Zur deutschen Auswahl aus Seinem
       Gesamtwerk" Weltstimmen [Stuttgart],
       XXIV, No. 6 (June), 260-262.
1050. Graves, Robert. Correspondence in The
       Times Literary Supplement (London),
       April 29, p. 209.
       [On "The Windhover"; reply to anon.
       rev. of Grigson, in TLS, March 18.]
1051. Grigson, Geoffrey. Gerard Manley Hopkins.
       (Writers and Their Work, No. 59.)
       London: Longmans, Green & Co.; 34 pp.
       1052. Anon. in The Times Literary Supplement
              (London), March 18, p. 165.
       1053. Devlin, Christopher, S.J. in The New
              Statesman and Nation, XLIX (March 26),
              447.
1054. Guidi, Augusto. "Milton e Hopkins,"
       English Miscellany [Rome], VI, 31-43.

1055. Haas, Willy. "Sprachschopfer, Philosoph, Priester: Das Gesamtwerk Gerard Manley Hopkins' in deutscher Auswahl," Englische Rundschau [Cologne], V, No. 23 (June 10), 306-307.
1056. Hazo, Samuel John. An Analysis of "Inscape" in the Poetry of Gerard Manley Hopkins. Unpublished M.A. thesis, Duquesne University.
1057. Hill, Archibald A. "An Analysis of 'The Windhover': An Experiment in Structural Method," Publications of the Modern Language Association of America, LXX, No. 5 (December), 968-978.
1058. Hohoff, Curt. "Hopkins, ein Dichter der Schöpfung," Hochland [Munich], XLVII, No. 5 (June), 424-431.
1059. Horst, Karl August. "Zuzang zu Hopkins," Wort und Wahrheit [Vienna], X, No. 9 (September), 716-719.
1060. Humiliata, Sister Mary. "Hopkins and the Prometheus Myth," Publications of the Modern Language Association of America, LXX, No. 1 (March), 58-68.
1061. Kornacki, Wanda Charlotte. Thomistic Principles of Esthetics in the Poetry of Gerard Manley Hopkins, Francis Thompson, and Coventry Patmore. Unpublished M.A. thesis, DePaul University.
1062. Miller, J. Hillis. "The Creation of the Self in Gerard Manley Hopkins," Journal of English Literary History, XXII, No. 4 (December), 293-319.
[959]. Morris, David. The Poetry of GMH and T. S. Eliot in the Light of the Donne Tradition. 1953.

1063. Sharrock, Roger. in The Modern Language Review, L, No. 2 (April), 242-243.

1064. Nolan, Gerald L. Correspondence in The Times Literary Supplement (London), June 24, p. 349. [On "The Windhover."]

1065. Nolan, Gerald L. Correspondence in The Times Literary Supplement (London), August 5, p. 445. [On "The Windhover."]

1066. Pennington, Frederic Adams. Gerard Manley Hopkins and Duns Scotus: The Derivation of Inscape and its Poetical Function. Unpublished M.A. thesis, Duke University.

1067. Phare, E. E. "Gerard Manley Hopkins and Richard Jefferies," Notes and Queries, n. s., II, No. 7 (July), 318.

[960]. Pick, John. A Hopkins Reader. 1953.

1068. Kelly, Hugh. in Studies, XLIV, No. 173 (Spring), 125-126.

1069. Pinto, V. de S. "Hopkins and 'The Trewnesse of the Christian Religion,'" The Times Literary Supplement (London), June 10, p. 317.

1070. Ritz, J. G. Correspondence in The Times Literary Supplement (London), May 6, p. 237. [On "The Windhover."]

1071. Rooney, William Joseph. "'Spelt from Sibly's Leaves'--A Study in Contrasting Methods of Evaluation," The Journal of Aesthetics & Art Criticism, XIII, No. 4 (June), 507-519.

1072. Rubenstein, Gladys. A Study of Gerard Manley Hopkins' Reputation as a Poet. Unpublished M.A. thesis, Claremont Graduate School.

1073. Smith, Robert Francis. A Comparative
       Study of Some Nature Poems of William
       Wordsworth and Gerard Manley Hopkins.
       Unpublished M.A. thesis, University
       of Notre Dame.
1074. Untermeyer, Louis. Makers of the Modern
       World. New York: Simon and Schuster,
       pp. 204-208.
1075. Ward, Dennis. "G. M. Hopkins: 'The
       Windhover: To Christ Our Lord,'" in
       Interpretations: Essays on Twelve
       English Poems, ed. John Wain. London:
       Routledge and K. Paul, pp. 138-152.
1076. Wasmuth, Ewald. "G. M. Hopkins' Asthetik,"
       Die Neue Rundschau [Berlin], LXVI,
       (Winter), 590-604.

                    1956
1077. Abbott, Claude Colleer. "Introduction,"
       Further Letters of Gerard Manley
       Hopkins including his Correspondence
       with Coventry Patmore. Second edition,
       revised. London: Oxford University
       Press, pp. xi-xliii,
    1078. Anon. in The Times Literary Supplement
           (London), December 21, p. 763.
    1079. Cockshut, A. O. J. in The Tablet, CCVIII
           (December 8), 500-502.
    1080. Hough, Graham. in The Spectator, CXCVII
           (December 28), 936-937.
    1081. Pick, John. in Renascence, VIII, No. 4
           (Summer), 216-217.
1082. Andrews, Robert F., O.S.A. An Explication
       of Gerard Manley Hopkins' "On a Piece
       of Music." Unpublished M.A. thesis, The
       Catholic University of America.
1083. Ayers, Robert W. "Hopkins' 'The Wind-
       hover': A Further Simplification,"
       Modern Language Notes, LXXI, No. 8
       (December), 577-584.

116   GERARD MANLEY HOPKINS

1084. Baird, Sister Mary Julian, R.S.M.
       "Blake, Hopkins, and Thomas Merton,"
       The Catholic World, CLXXXIII (April),
       46-49.
[993]. Clemen, W. and U. Gerard Manley Hopkins:
       Gedichte. 1954.
       1085. Bretelle, Leon. in Die Kirche in der
             Welt [Munich], VIII, No. 2, 241-242.
1086. Conlon, Sister M. Brendan. The Fire
       Image in the Poetry of Gerard Manley
       Hopkins. Unpublished M.A. thesis, The
       Creighton University.
1087. Doyle, Francis G., S.J. "A Note on
       Hopkins's Windhover," Studies, XLV,
       No. 177 (Spring), 88-91.
1088. Duncan-Jones, E. E. "R. W. Dixon's
       'Terrible Crystal,'" Notes and
       Queries, n. s., III, No. 6 (June),
       267.
1089. Farrell, Melvin Lloyd. The Significance
       of Christ in the Poetry of Gerard
       Manley Hopkins. Unpublished M.A.
       thesis, University of Washington.
1090. Giovannini, Margaret. "Hopkins' 'The
       Caged Skylark,'" The Explicator, XIV,
       No. 6 (March), item 35.
1091. Heights [Manila], V, No. 1 (July). "A
       Jesuit Poet":
       Ayala, Antonio V. "The Problem of
       Suffering," 75-79.
       Dualan, Jesús P. "Hope and Desolation,"
       73-74.
       Mapa, Dionisio L. "Hopkins and Prag-
       matism," 63-65.
       Paterno, Roberto. "The 'In-Between'
       Being," 67-71.
       Romualdez, Antonio V. "That Being In-
       doors Dwells," 59-61.
       Severine, Rodolfo, Jr. "Echoes," 81-84.

1092. Holloway, Sister Marcella M., C.S.J.
"Hopkins' 'Sonnet 65 (No Worst, There
is None),'" The Explicator, XIV, No.
8 (May), item 51.
1093. Jankowsky, Kurt. Die Versauffassung bei
Gerard Manley Hopkins, den Imagisten
und T. S. Eliot. Unpublished Ph.D.
dissertation, University of Munich.
1094. Kelly, Hugh. "The Windhover--and
Christ," Studies, XLV, No. 178
(Summer), 188-193.
1095. King, Anne R. "Hopkins' 'Windhover' and
Blake," English Studies, XXXVII, No.
6, 245-252.
1096. Lloyd-Jones, Richard. Common Speech:
A Poetic Effect for Hopkins, Browning,
and Arnold. Unpublished Ph.D. disser-
tation, University of Iowa.
[In Dissertation Abstracts, XVI, No.
5 (May), 957.]
1097. Melchiori, Giorgio. "Two Mannerists:
James and Hopkins," The Tightrope
Walkers: Studies of Mannerism in
Modern English Literature. London:
Routledge & Kegan Paul, pp. 13-33.
1098. Paye, Sister Mary Paul, R.S.M. The
Logical Structure of the Sonnets of
Gerard Manley Hopkins. Unpublished
M.A. thesis, The Catholic University of
America.
1099. Pick, John. "Gerard Manley Hopkins," in
The Victorian Poets: A Guide to
Research, ed. Frederic E. Faverty.
Cambridge, Massachusetts: Harvard
University Press, pp. 196-227.
1100. Ritz, Jean-Georges. "'The Windhover' de
G. M. Hopkins," Etudes Anglaises,
IX, No. 1 (January-March), 14-22.

1101.   Schoeck, R. J. "Influence and Origi-
          nality in the Poetry of Hopkins,"
          Renascence, IX, No. 2 (Winter), 77-84.
1102.   Sherwood, H. C. "Hopkins' 'Spelt from
          Sibyl's Leaves,'" The Explicator,
          XV, No. 1 (October), item 5.
1103.   Spira, Theodor. "Gerard Manley Hopkins:
          Zu einer deutschen Neuerscheinung,"
          Anglia [Tübingen], LXXIV, No. 3,
          333-344.
1104.   Tillotson, Geoffrey. Correspondence in
          The Times Literary Supplement (London),
          January 6, p. 7.
1105.   Weatherhead, A. Kingsley. "G. M. Hopkins:
          'The Windhover,'" Notes and Queries,
          n. s., III, No. 8 (August), 354.
1106.   Whitlock, Baird W. "Gerard Hopkins'
          'Windhover,'" Notes and Queries, n.
          s., III, No. 4 (April), 169-171.

                    1957
[1077].   Abbott, Claude Colleer. Further
            Letters of GMH. 1956.
     1107.   Allen, Louis. in The Durham University
               Journal, n. s., XVIII, No 3 (June),
               136-137.
     1108.   Ames, Ruth. in The Catholic World,
               CLXXV (May), 155.
     1109.   Anon. in The Quarterly Review, CCXCV,
               No. 613 (July), 363-364.
     1110.   Armstrong, Robert. in The Poetry Review,
               XLVIII, No. 2 (April-June), 109.
     1111.   Birrell, T. A. in English Studies
               [Amsterdam], XXXVIII, No. 5 (October),
               225-226.
     1112.   Bischoff, Anthony, S.J. in Thought,
               XXXII, No. 126 (Autumn), 455-457.
     1113.   Cockshut, A. O. J. in The Manchester
               Guardian, January 1, p. 3.

1114. D., N. K. in San Francisco Chronicle,
        "This World" supplement, February 24,
        p. 22.
1115. Devlin, Christopher. in The Month, n.
        s., XVII, No. 5 (May), 332-333.
1116. Gillet, Eric. in The National and English
        Review, CXLVIII, No. 888 (February),
        87.
1117. Kelly, Hugh. in Studies, XLV, No. 181
        (Spring), 121-123.
1118. Miller, Betty. in The Twentieth Century,
        CLXI, No. 961 (March), 306-308.
1119. Pick, John. in Victorian Studies, I,
        No. 1 (September), 91-93.
1120. Abbott, C. Colleer. "Further Letters of
        G. M. Hopkins," The Times Literary
        Supplement (London), February 1, p.
        65.
1121. Aronowitz, Herbert. The Relationship of
        the Spiritual Exercises of St.
        Ignatius to the Poetry of Gerard
        Manley Hopkins as Evidenced in "The
        Wreck of the Deutschland." Un-
        published B.A. thesis, Rutgers, The
        State University.
1122. Bischoff, A., S.J. Correspondence in
        The Times Literary Supplement (Lon-
        don), June 7, p. 349.
        [On Hopkins' Spiritual Diaries.]
1123. Boyle, Robert R., S.J. "A Christmas
        Poem: By Father Gerard Hopkins, S.J.,"
        The Queen's Work, L, No. 3 (December),
        18-19.
1124. Coanda, Richard. "Hopkins and Donne:
        'Mystic' and Metaphysical," Rena-
        scence, IX, No. 4 (Summer), 180-187.

1125. Connor, Sister Juanita Maria, S.S.J.
       The Relationship of Gerard Manley
       Hopkins and his Life of Consecration.
       Unpublished M.A. thesis, Villanova
       University.
1126. Donovan, Mother Mary Inez. The Aesthetics
       of Gerard Manley Hopkins, S.J. Un-
       published M.A. thesis, University of
       Detroit.
1127. Frankenburg, Lloyd [and others]. in
       The New York Times Book Review,
       November 10, p. 34.
       [Reply to Peel, in NYTBR, October 20.]
1128. Gallo, Ernest Anthony. Gerard Manley
       Hopkins: Linguistic Innovator.
       Unpublished M.A. thesis, New York
       University.
1129. Gardner, W. H. Correspondence in The
       Times Literary Supplement (London),
       March 29, p. 193.

       [On Hopkins' Spiritual Diaries.]
1130. Guzie, Tad W., S.J. "Are Modern Poets
       Morbid?" The Catholic World, CLXXXV
       (April), 26-32.
1131. Harrison, Thomas P. "The Birds of
       Gerard Manley Hopkins," Studies in
       Philology, LIV, No. 3 (July), 448-463.
1132. Leyris, Pierre. Gerard Manley Hopkins:
       "Reliquiae." Vers, Proses, Dessins,
       réunis et traduits. Paris: Editions
       du Seuil.
       1133. Valette, Jacques. in Mercure de France,
             CCCXXXI (December 1), 696.
1134. Lisca, Peter. "The Return of 'The Wind-
       hover,'" College English, XIX, No. 3
       (December), 124-126.
1135. Litzinger, Boyd. "Hopkins' 'The Habit
       of Perfection,'" The Explicator, XVI,
       No. 1 (October), item 1.

1136. Martin, Philip M. Mastery and Mercy:
       A Study of Two Religious Poems, "The
       Wreck of the Deutschland" by G. M.
       Hopkins and "Ash Wednesday" by T. S.
       Eliot. London: Oxford University
       Press; xii, 149 pp.
       1137. Anon. in The Times Literary Supplement
              (London), June 28, p. 398.
1138. Matchett, William H. "An Analysis of
       'The Windhover,'" Publications of
       the Modern Language Association of
       America, LXXII, No. 1 (March), 310-
       311.
1139. Miles, Josephine. "Hopkins: The Sweet
       and Lovely Language," Eras and Modes
       in English Poetry. Berkeley: Uni-
       versity of California Press, pp. 164-
       177.
1140. Nowell-Smith, Simon. "Bridges, Hopkins,
       and Dr. Daniel," The Times Literary
       Supplement (London), December 13,
       p. 764.
1141. Peel, J. H. B. "The Echoes in the Boom-
       ing Voice," The New York Times Book
       Review, October 20, pp. 40-41.
       [On Hopkins and Dylan Thomas.]
1142. Ratliff, John D. "Hopkins' 'The May
       Magnificat,' 19-22," The Explicator,
       XVI, No. 3 (December), item 17.
[990]. Reeves, James. Selected Poems of GMH.
       1953.
       1143. C., M. M. in Dominicana, XLII, No. 4
              (December), 369-370.
1144. Sieveking, Lance. "Remembering Gerard
       Manley Hopkins," The Listener, LVII
       (January), 151-152.
1145. Sieveking, Lance. "Gerard Manley Hopkins,"
       The Eye of the Beholder. London:
       Hutton Press, pp. 275-285.

1146. Whelan, Rosalie C. The Critical Recep-
       tion of the First and Second Editions
       of the Poems of Gerard Manley Hopkins.
       Unpublished M.A. thesis, Marquette
       University.

                        1958
[1077]. Abbot, Claude Colleer. Further Letters
         of GMH. 1956.
       1147. Moore, Rosalie. in Poetry, XCII, No. 2
              (May), 113-115.
       1148. Phillipson, Dom Wulstan. in The Down-
              side Review, LXXVI, No. 246 (Autumn),
              402-410.
       1149. Rillie, John A. M. in The Review of
              English Studies, n. s., IX, No. 35,
              334-336.
       1150. Weyand, Norman, S.J. in Renascence, XI,
              No. 1 (Autumn), 53-56.
1151. Bischoff, A. "Gerard Manley Hopkins,"
       Victorian Newsletter, No. 13 (Spring),
       pp. 23-24.
1152. Brinlee, Robert Washington. The Religion
       and Poetic Theory of Gerard Manley
       Hopkins. Unpublished M.A. thesis,
       University of Tulsa.
1153. Gibson, Walker. "Sound and Sense in
       G. M. Hopkins," Modern Language Notes,
       LXXIII, No. 2 (February), 95-100.
1154. Heuser, Alan. The Shaping Vision of
       Gerard Manley Hopkins. London and
       New York: Oxford University Press;
       viii, 128 pp.
     1155. Anon. in The Times Literary Supplement
            (London), October 17, p. 594.
1156. Joselyn, Sister M., O.S.B. "Herbert and
       Hopkins: Two Lyrics," Renascence, X,
       No. 4 (Summer), 192-195.
       ["Affliction (1)" and "Carrion Comfort."]

1157. Kelly, John C. "Gerard Manley Hopkins: Piety versus Poetry," Studies, XLVII (Winter), 421-430.

1158. Kissane, James. "Classical Echoes in Hopkins' 'Heaven-Haven,'" Modern Language Notes, LXXIII, No. 7 (November), 491-492.

[1132]. Leyris, Pierre. Gerard Manley Hopkins: "Reliquiae." 1957.

    1159. Anon. in The Times Literary Supplement (London), April 4, p. 184.

    1160. Mambrino, Jean. in Etudes, CCXCVII, No. 4 (April), 136-137.

    1161. Thomas, Henri. in La Nouvelle Revue Française, VI, No. 61 (January 1), 122-125.

1162. Magny, Olivier de. "Gérard Manley Hopkins et le Coeur des Choses," Les Lettres Nouvelles, VI, No. 57 (February), 248-256.

1163. Mellown, E. W. The Reception of Gerard Manley Hopkins' Poems, 1909-1957. Unpublished M.A. thesis, University of London.

1164. Northup, Eileen Bernice O'Reilly. Hopkins as a Student of Pater. Unpublished M.A. thesis, University of Rhode Island.

1165. Ritz, J.-G. "Un Poète Anglais: Le R. P. Gérard Manley Hopkins, S.J.," Le Bulletin des Lettres [Lyon], XX, No. 198 (May 15), 189-196.

1166. Schneider, Elisabeth. "Hopkins' 'The Wreck of the Deutschland,' Stanza 33," The Explicator, XVI, No. 8 (May), item 46.

1167.   Stanzel, Franz. "G. M. Hopkins, W. B.
        Yeats, D. H. Lawrence, und die
        Spontaneität der Dichtung," in
        Anglistische Studien, ed. Friedrich
        Wild. (Wiener Beiträge zur Englischen
        Philologie, LXVI.) Wien: W. Braumüller,
        pp. 179-193.
1168.   Storey, Graham. "The Notebooks and
        Papers of Gerard Manley Hopkins: A
        New Edition," The Month, n. s., XX,
        No. 5 (November), 273-281.
1169.   Swanzy, Annabeth. A Study of Gerard
        Manley Hopkins' Poetic Theory and
        Practice. Unpublished M.A. thesis,
        Louisiana State University.
1170.   Vogelgesang, John. "Hopkins' Sonnet to
        R. B.," Philippine Studies, VI, No.
        3 (August), 315-324.

                        1959
1171.   Abraham, John August. Hopkins and Scotus:
        An Analogy Between Inscape and Indi-
        viduation. Unpublished Ph.D. disser-
        tation, University of Wisconsin.
1172.   Allison, Alexander W. "Hopkins' 'I Wake
        and Feel the Fell of Dark,'" The
        Explicator, XVII, No. 8 (May), item
        54.
1173.   Assad, Thomas J. "A Closer Look at
        Hopkins' 'Carrion Comfort,'" Tulane
        Studies in English, IX, 91-102.
1174.   Baum, Paull F. "Sprung Rhythm," Pub-
        lications of the Modern Language
        Association of America, LXXIV, No. 4
        (September), 418-425.
1175.   Bell, Sister Ann Charles, S.N.D. Gerard
        Manley Hopkins and the Mystical Life.
        Unpublished M.A. thesis, Villanova
        University.

1176. Blume, Bernhard. "Sein und Scheitern:
zur Geschichte einer Metapher,"
Germanisch-Romanische Monatsschrift,
n. s., IX, No. 3 (July), 277-287.
1177. Bowen, Robert O. "Scotism in Gerard
Manley Hopkins," History of Ideas
Newsletter, V, No. 1 (Winter), 11-14.
1178. Britton, John, S.J. "'Pied Beauty' and
the Glory of God," Renascence, XI,
No. 2 (Winter), 72-75.
1179. Buggy, Sister James Marita, I.H.M.
Growth of the Literary Reputation of
Gerard Manley Hopkins. Unpublished
M.A. thesis, Villanova University.
1180. Cascio, Joseph E., Jr. Gerard Manley
Hopkins and the Arts of Literary
Criticism, Painting, and Music. Unpublished M.A. thesis, Saint John's
University.
1181. Corke, Hilary. "A Housecarl in Loyola's
Menie," Encounter, XII, No. 5 (May),
63-67.
1182. Devlin, Christopher, S.J. "Introduction[s]," The Sermons and Devotional Writings of Gerard Manley
Hopkins. London: Oxford University
Press, pp. xiii-xiv, 3-12, 107-121,
213-221.
1183. Anon. in Letters and Notices, LXIV,
No. 318 (July), 104-109.
1184. Abbott, C. Colleer. in The Listener,
LXI (March 12), 476, 479.
1185. [Bischoff, D. A.]. in The Times
Literary Supplement (London),
September 25, p. 544.
1186. Busby, Christopher. in The Dublin Review, CCXXXIII, No. 480 (Summer),
183-190.

1187. Jones, John. in The New Statesman, LVII
       (March 7), 338-339.
1188. Kelly, John C. in Studies, XLVIII, No.
       190 (Summer), 226-230.
1189. Meath, Gerard, O.P. in The Tablet,
       CCXIII (February 14), 154-155.
1190. Morse, Samuel French. in The New York
       Times Book Review, April 5, pp. 4-5.
1191. Pick, John. in Modern Philology, LVII,
       No. 2 (November), 137-138.
1192. Robson, W. W. in The Spectator, CCII
       (February 27), 300.
1193. Downes, David A. Gerard Manley Hopkins:
       A Study of His Ignatian Spirit. New
       York: Bookman Associates; 195 pp.
1194. Goodin, George. "Man and Nature in
       Hopkins' 'Ribblesdale,'" Notes and
       Queries, n. s., VI, No. 11 (December),
       453-454.
[1154]. Heuser, Alan. The Shaping Spirit of
       GMH. 1958.
1195. Anon. in College English, XXI, No. 2
       (November), 113-114.
1196. Gardner, W. H. in The Modern Language
       Review, LIV, No. 3 (July), 424-425.
1197. Hardy, John Edward. in The Yale Review,
       XLVIII, No. 3 (March), 410-411.
1198. Lougheed, W. C. in Queen's Quarterly,
       LXVI, No. 1 (Spring), 173-174.
1199. McDonnell, Thomas P. in The Catholic
       World, CLXXXIX (May), 174-175.
1200. Park, B. A. in Books Abroad, XXXIII,
       No. 3 (Summer), 351.
1201. Pick, John. in America, C, No. 14
       (January 10), 431.
1202. Pick, John. in Modern Philology, LVI,
       No. 4 (May), 282-283.
1203. Stanford, Derek. in English, XII, No.
       70 (Spring), 146-148.

1204. Hohoff, Curt. "Hopkins, ein Dichter der
       Schöpfung," in Lob der Schöpfung und
       Argernis der Zeit: Moderne Christliche
       in Kritik und Deutung, ed. Karlheinz
       Schmidthüs. Fribourg: Herder-
       Bücherei, pp. 101-109.
       [Reprinted from Hochland, June, 1955.]
1205. Howarth, R. G. "An Unconscious Prophet
       of Hopkins," Notes and Queries, n. s.,
       VI, No. 11 (December), 443-444.
1206. Johnson, W. Stacey. "The Imagery of
       Gerard Manley Hopkins," Victorian
       Newsletter, No. 16 (Fall), pp. 18-23.
1207. Lenz, Sister Mary Baylon. The Meditative
       Style in Gerard Manley Hopkins. Un-
       published M.A. thesis, University of
       Notre Dame.
1208. Litzinger, Boyd. "Hopkins' 'The Wreck
       of the Deutschland,' Stanza 33," The
       Explicator, XVIII, No. 3 (December),
       item 19.
1209. Mann, John S. A Study in the Relation
       of Structure to Thought in the Poetry
       of Gerard Manley Hopkins. Unpub-
       lished M.A. thesis, Columbia Univer-
       sity.
1210. McBrien, William A. Likeness in the
       Theses and Prosody of Gerard Manley
       Hopkins and Dylan Thomas. Unpub-
       lished Ph.D. dissertation, Saint
       John's University.
1211. Mellown, Elgin W. "Gerard Manley Hopkins
       and His Public, 1889-1918," Modern
       Philology, LVII, No. 2 (November),
       94-99.
1212. Mellown, Elgin W. "Hopkins, Hall Caine,
       and D. G. Rossetti," Notes and Queries,
       n. s., VI, No. 3 (March), 109-110.

1213. Nowell-Smith, Simon. "Housman In-
scriptions," The Times Literary
Supplement (London), November 6,
p. 643.
1214. Pearson, W. H. "G. M. Hopkins and
'Gifted Hopkins,'" Notes and Queries,
n. s., VI, No. 11 (December), 452-
453.
1215. Rathmell, J. C. A. "Explorations and
Recoveries--Hopkins, Ruskin and the
Sidney Psalter," The London Magazine,
VI, No. 9 (September), 51-66.
1216. Scheve, Brother Adelbert, F.S.C.
"Hopkins' 'The Wreck of the Deutsch-
land,' Stanza 33," The Explicator,
XVII, No. 9 (June), item 60.
1217. Schoeck, R. J. "Peine Forte et dure and
Hopkins' 'Margaret Clitheroe,'"
Modern Language Notes, LXXIV, No. 3
(March), 220-224.
1218. Shkolnick, Sylvia. Gerard Manley Hopkins:
A Study in the Poetry of Meditation.
Unpublished M.A. thesis, Columbia
University.
1219. Silverstein, Henry. On Tom's Garland.
Unpublished M.A. thesis, New York
University.
1220. Stephenson, A. A., S.J. "G. M. Hopkins
and John Donne," The Downside Review,
LXXVII, No. 249 (Summer-Autumn),
300-320.
2121. Stillinger, Jack. "Hopkins' 'Skates
Heel' in 'The Windhover,'" Notes and
Queries, n. s., VI, No. 6 (June),
215-216.
1222. Storey, Graham. "Preface," The Journals
and Papers of Gerard Manley Hopkins.
London: Oxford University Press,
pp. ix-xxxii.

[1183]. Anon. in Letters and Notices, LXIV, No. 318 (July), 104-109.

[1184]. Abbott, C. Colleer. in The Listener, LXI (March 12), 476-479.

[1185]. [Bischoff, D. A.]. in The Times Literary Supplement (London), September 25, p. 544.

[1186]. Busby, Christopher. in The Dublin Review, CCXXXIII, No. 480 (Summer), 183-190.

1223. Evans, Illtud, O.P. in Blackfriars, XL, No. 471 (June), 270-273.

1224. Gillet, Eric. in The National and English Review, CLII, No. 914 (April) 150.

[1187]. Jones, John. in The New Statesman, LVII (March 7), 338-339.

[1188]. Kelly, John C. in Studies, XLVIII, No. 190 (Summer), 226-230.

[1189]. Meath, Gerard, O.P. in The Tablet, CCXIII (February 14), 154-155.

[1190]. Morse, Samuel French. in The New York Times Book Review, April 5, pp. 4-5

1225. Park, B. A. in Books Abroad, XXXIII, No. 4 (Autumn), 461.

1226. Robie, Burton A. in Library Journal, LXXXIV, No. 7 (April 1), 1133-1134.

[1192]. Robson, W. W. in The Spectator, CCII (February 27), 300.

1227. Valette, Jacques. in Mercure de France, CCCXXXVI (June 1), 337.

1228. Wain, John. in New York Herald Tribune Weekly Book Review, March 15, p. 8.

1229. Sumner, C. "Gerard Manley Hopkins: Twenty-five Poems Written 1860-1875," Centre Marial Canadien [Nicolet, Quebec], Tract No. 98 (April), pp.5-40.

1230. Thérèse, Sister, S.N.D. "Hopkins'
       'Spelt from Sibyl's Leaves,'" The
       Explicator, XVII, No. 7 (April),
       item 45.
1231. Wain, John. Gerard Manley Hopkins: An
       Idiom of Desperation. (Chatterton
       Lecture on An English Poet, British
       Academy, read 13 May.) London:
       Oxford University Press.
1232. Young, Lillian. The "Maker" and His
       Maker: A Study of the Conflict Be-
       tween the Devotion to Art and to God
       in Michelangelo, Donne, and Hopkins
       as a Background for Their Religious
       Sonnets. Unpublished M.A. thesis,
       Cornell University.

                    1960
1233. Altick, Richard D. "Four Victorian Poets
       and an Exploding Island," Victorian
       Studies, III, No. 3 (March), 249-260.
1234. Beauregard, David Napoleon. The
       Aesthetic Theory of Gerard Manley
       Hopkins. Unpublished M.A. thesis,
       Ohio State University.
1235. Boyle, Robert. "Hopkins' Imagery: The
       Thread for the Maze," Thought, XXXV,
       No. 136 (Spring), 57-90.
[1182]. Devlin, Christopher, S.J. The Sermons
       and Devotional Writings of GMH.
       1959.
       1236. Hill, A. G. in Essays in Criticism, X,
              No. 2 (April), 215-219.
       1237. Ong, Walter J. in Victorian Studies,
              III, No. 3 (March), 305-308.
       1238. Phillipson, Dom Wulstan. in The Down-
              side Review, LXXVIII, No. 252
              (Summer), 213-217.

1239. Stanford, Derek. in The Month, n. s.,
        XXIV, No. 3 (September), 158-164.
1240. Westrup, J. A. in Music and Letters,
        XLI, No. 1 (January), 74-75.
[1193]. Downes, David A. GMH: A Study of
        His Ignatian Spirit. 1959.
1241. Heuser, Alan. in Queen's Quarterly,
        LXVII, No. 3 (Autumn), 492.
[1154]. Heuser, Alan. The Shaping Vision of
        GMH. 1958.
1242. Moore, Carlisle. in Comparative Litera-
        ture, XII, No. 2 (Spring), 172-175.
[1237]. Ong, Walter J. in Victorian Studies,
        III, No. 3 (March), 305-308.
1243. Jennings, Elizabeth. "The Unity of
        Incarnation: A Study of Gerard
        Manley Hopkins," The Dublin Review,
        CCXXXIV, No. 484 (Summer), 170-184.
1244. Lackamp, John Jerome, S.J. The Influ-
        ence of Music on the Life of Gerard
        Manley Hopkins. Unpublished M.A.
        thesis, Loyola University [Chicago].
1245. Lawler, Donald L. Gerard Manley Hopkins:
        Three Patterns of his Poetry. Unpub-
        lished M.A. thesis, Columbia Univer-
        sity.
1246. Litzinger, Boyd. "The Genesis of
        Hopkins' 'Heaven-Haven,'" Victorian
        Newsletter, No. 17 (Spring), pp. 31-
        33.
1247. Mooney, Stephen. "Hopkins and Counter-
        point," Victorian Newsletter, No. 18
        (Fall), pp. 21-22.
1248. Morati, Luciano. "Spiritualità e
        Ispirazione nella Poesia di Gerard
        Manley Hopkins," Letture [Milan],
        XV, No. 8-9 (August-September), 563-
        570.

1249. O'Brien, A. P. "Structure Complex of
       Hopkins's Words," The Indian Journal
       of English Studies, No. 1, pp. 48-56.
1250. Ritz, Jean-Georges. Robert Bridges and
       Gerard Hopkins, 1863-1889: A
       Literary Friendship. London: Oxford
       University Press; xvii, 182 pp.
   1251. Anon. in The Times Literary Supplement
          (London), May 6, p. 288.
   1252. Pinto, V. de S. in The Critical Quarterly,
          II, No. 3 (Autumn), 281-282.
   1253. Reeves, James. in The New Statesman,
          LIX (May 14), 724.
   1254. Reid, J. C. in Victorian Studies, IV,
          No. 2 (December), 182-183.
   [1239]. Stanford, Derek. in The Month, n. s.,
            XXIV, No. 3 (September), 158-164.
1255. Schneider, Elisabeth. "Hopkins' 'The
       Windhover,'" The Explicator, XVIII,
       No. 4 (January), item 22.
1256. Schreiber, Annette Claire. Hopkins'
       "The Wreck of the Deutschland": A
       Study. Unpublished Ph.D. disserta-
       tion, Cornell University.
[1222]. Storey, Graham. The Journals and
         Papers of GMH. 1959.
   [1236]. Hill, A. G. in Essays in Criticism,
            X, No. 2 (April), 215-219.
   [1237]. Ong, Walter J. in Victorian Studies,
            III, No. 3 (March), 305-308.
   [1238]. Phillipson, Dom Wulstan. in The Down-
            side Review, LXXVIII, No. 252
            (Summer), 213-217.
   [1239]. Stanford, Derek. in The Month, n. s.,
            XXIV, No. 3 (September), 158-164.
   1257. Ure, Peter. in The Review of English
          Studies, n. s., XI, No. 44, 445-447.
1258. Walsh, William. "G. M. Hopkins and a
       Sense of the Particular," The Use of
       Imagination: Educational Thought and
       the Literary Mind. London: Chatto
       & Windus, pp. 121-136.

1259. Wayman, D. G. "Mary and Two Poets,"
       The Cord, X, No. 4 (April), 121-124.

                          1961
1260. Assad, Thomas J. "Hopkins' 'The Wind-
       hover,'" Tulane Studies in English,
       XI, 87-95.
1261. Boyle, Robert, S.J. Metaphor in Hopkins.
       Chapel Hill, North Carolina: Uni-
       versity of North Carolina Press; xxiv,
       231 pp.
    1262. Robie, Burton A. in Library Journal,
           LXXXVI, No. 16 (September 15), 2945.
    1263. Teeling, John. in America, CVI, No. 2
           (October 14), 50-51.
1264. Brophy, James. "The Noble Brute:
       Medieval Nuance in 'The Windhover,'"
       Modern Language Notes, LXXVI, No. 8
       (December), 673-674.
1265. Brown, T. J. "English Literary Auto-
       graphs XXXIX: Gerard Manley Hopkins,
       1844-1889," The Book Collector, X,
       No. 3 (Autumn), 321.
1266. Conlon, Michael J. A Bibliography of
       the Writings and Ana of Gerard Manley
       Hopkins from January 1, 1947 to
       January 1, 1958. Unpublished M.A.
       thesis, University of Kentucky.
[1182]. Devlin, Christopher, S.J. The Sermons
       and Devotional Writings of GMH. 1959.
    1267. Gardner, W. H. in The Month, n. s.,
           XXV, No. 2 (February), 82-95.
    1268. Litzinger, Boyd. in Cithara, I, No. 1
           (November), 48-50.
1269. Downes, David A. "The Hopkins Enigma,"
       Thought, XXXVI, No. 143 (Winter),
       573-594.

1270. Gardner, W. H. Correspondence in The
       Times Literary Supplement (London),
       August 18, p. 549.
       [On Bridges' "debt" to Hopkins.]
1271. Guardini, Romano. "Asthetisch-theo-
       logische Gedanken zu G. M. Hopkins'
       Sonnett 'Der Turmfalke,'" in
       Unterscheidung und Bewahrung:
       Festschrift für Hermann Kunisch, eds.
       Klaus Lazarowicz and Wolfgang Kron.
       Berlin: Walter de Gruyter & Co.,
       pp. 170-174.
1272. Joshi, B. N. "Hopkins and T. S. Eliot--
       A Study in Linguistic Innovation,"
       Osmania Journal of English Studies,
       No. 1, pp. 13-16.
1273. Kelly, Richard Michael. The Intellectual
       Milieu of Gerard Manley Hopkins.
       Unpublished M.A. thesis, Duke Univer-
       sity.
1274. Lenz, Mildred. A Poet's View of Reality:
       A Study of the Works of Gerard Manley
       Hopkins. Unpublished M.A. thesis,
       University of Kansas.
1275. Litzinger, Boyd A. "Hopkins' 'Pied
       Beauty' Once More," Renascence, XIII,
       No. 3 (Spring), 136-138.
1276. Litzinger, Boyd A. "Hopkins' 'The Wreck
       of the Deutschland,' Stanza 19," The
       Explicator, XX, No. 1 (September),
       item 7.
1277. Mackenzie, Norman. Correspondence in
       The Times Literary Supplement (Lon-
       don), September 1, p. 588.
       [On Bridges' "debt" to Hopkins.]
1278. Markert, Marilyn Rese. Gerard Manley
       Hopkins' Use of Sonnet Form. Unpub-
       lished M.A. thesis, John Carroll
       University.

1279. McDonnell, Thomas P. "Hopkins as a
      Sacramental Poet: A Reply to Yvor
      Winters," Renascence, XIV, No. 1
      (Autumn), 25-33, 41.
1280. McLaughlin, Rev. John Joseph, S.J. The
      Influence of St. Paul on Gerard Manley
      Hopkins. Unpublished M.A. thesis,
      Boston College.
1281. Miller, J. Hillis. "'Orion' in 'The
      Wreck of the Deutschland,'" Modern
      Language Notes, LXXVI, No. 6 (June),
      509-514.
1282. Müller-Schwefe, Gerhard. "G. M. Hopkins--
      der Victorianer," Festschrift zum 75:
      Geburtstag von Theodor Spira, ed.
      H[elmut] Viebrock and W[illi]
      Erzgräber. Heidelberg: Univer-
      stätsverlag, pp. 233-239.
1283. Napier, Murray Patrick. A Study from
      the Sermons of Gerard Manley Hopkins.
      Unpublished M.A. thesis, McGill
      University.
1284. Nist, John. "Gerard Manley Hopkins and
      Textural Intensity: A Linguistic
      Analysis," College English, XXII,
      No. 7 (April), 497-500.
1285. Norris, Carolyn Brimley. Rhetoric and
      Poetic Language in the Sermons of
      Gerard Manley Hopkins. Unpublished
      M.A. thesis, University of Tennessee.
1286. Nowell-Smith, Simon. Correspondence in
      The Times Literary Supplement (London),
      May 12, p. 293.
      [On Bridges' "debt" to Hopkins.]
1287. Onesta, P. A. "The Self in Hopkins,"
      English Studies in Africa [Johannes-
      burg], IV, No. 2 (September), 174-181.

1288. Ong, Walter J, S.J. "Hopkins: Not For
      Burning," College English, XXIII, No.
      1 (October), 60.
      [Reply to Nist, in College English,
      April.]
1289. Parker, Dorothy Elizabeth Hagman.
      Gerard Manley Hopkins and the Critics.
      Unpublished Ph.D. dissertation, Uni-
      versity of Texas.
      [In Dissertation Abstracts, XXII, No.
      1 (July), 263.]
1290. Pocs, John A. Nationalism in the Poetry
      of Gerard Manley Hopkins. Unpub-
      lished M.A. thesis, Bowling Green
      State University.
1291. Rader, Louis. The Dark Sonnets of
      Gerard Manley Hopkins. Unpublished
      M.A. thesis, Cornell University.
1292. Riordan, Mary Marguerite. A Study of
      the Similarities in the Works of
      Gerard Manley Hopkins and Walt Whit-
      man. Unpublished M.A. thesis, San
      Francisco State College.
1293. Ritz, J. G. Correspondence in The Times
      Literary Supplement (London), June
      30, p. 480.
      [On Bridges' "debt" to Hopkins.]
1294. Roeder, Raymond L., Jr. The Sonnet
      Tradition and Gerard Manley Hopkins.
      Unpublished senior thesis, University
      of Santa Clara.
[1222]. Storey, Graham. The Journals and
      Papers of GMH. 1959.
      1295. Gardner, W. H. in The Month, n. s.,
             XXV, No. 2 (January), 34-47.
      [1268]. Litzinger, Boyd. in Cithara, I, No. 1
             (November), 48-50.

1296. Sutherland, Donald. "Hopkins Again,"
       Prairie Schooner, XXXV, No. 3 (Fall),
       197-242.
1297. Thomas, J. D. "Hopkins' 'The Windhover,'"
       The Explicator, XX, No. 4 (December),
       item 31.
1298. Tillotson, Geoffrey. Correspondence in
       The Times Literary Supplement (Lon-
       don), June 30, p. 480.
       [On Bridges' "debt" to Hopkins.]
1299. Turner, Edmond Glen. A Study of Dialect
       in the Poetry of Gerard Manley
       Hopkins. Unpublished M.A. thesis,
       University of Idaho.
1300. Zelocchi, Rosanna. "La 'barbarica
       bellezza' di Gerard Manley Hopkins,"
       Convivium [Turin], XXIX, No. 3 (May-
       June), 461-471.

                        1962
1301. Ames, Charlotte. "God's Grandeur":
       The Image and Effect. Unpublished
       M.A. thesis, The Catholic University of
       America.
1302. Barnes, Roslyn Tennie. Gerard Manley
       Hopkins and Pierre Teilhard de
       Chardin: A Formulation of Mysticism
       for a Scientific Age. Unpublished
       M.A. thesis, University of Iowa.
1303. Bender, Todd Kay. Some Derivative
       Elements in the Poetry of Gerard
       Manley Hopkins. Unpublished Ph.D.
       dissertation, Stanford University.
       [In Dissertation Abstracts, XXIII,
       No. 11 (May, 1963), 4352.]
1304. Bernad, Miguel A. "Hopkins' 'Pied
       Beauty': A Note on Its Ignatian
       Inspiration," Essays in Criticism,
       XII, No. 2 (April), 217-220.

[1261]. Boyle, Robert. Metaphor in Hopkins.
         1961.
         1305. Gardner, W. H. in The Modern Language
                Review, LVII, No. 4 (October), 600-
                601.
         1306. Gibson, Walker. in Victorian Studies,
                V, No. 4 (June), 353.
         1307. Hemphill, George. in College English,
                XXIII, No. 6 (March), 514.
         1308. Heuser, Alan. in Queen's Quarterly,
                LXIX, No. 2 (Summer), 323.
         1309. Stallknecht, Newton P. in The Yale
                Review, LI, No. 4 (Summer), 637-642.
1310. Brennan, Norman Charles. An Objective
       Interpretation of Three Mature
       Sonnets of Gerard Manley Hopkins.
       Unpublished M.A. thesis, Niagara
       University.
1311. Cleary, Helen Kae. In His Own Image:
       A Study of Hopkins' Poetic Treatment
       of Man. Unpublished M.A. thesis,
       Cornell University.
[1182]. Devlin, Christopher, S.J. The Sermons
         and Devotional Writings of GMH.
         1959.
         1312. Duncan-Jones, E. E. in The Modern Lan-
                guage Review, LVII, No. 3 (July),
                431-433.
1313. Eleanor, Mother Mary, S.H.C.J. "Hopkins'
       'Windhover' and Southwell's Hawk,"
       Renascence, XV, No. 1 (Fall), 21-22,
       27.
1314. Evarts, Prescott, Jr. Inscape and
       Symbol in the Poetry of Gerard
       Manley Hopkins. Unpublished M.A.
       thesis, Columbia University.

CRITICISM OF THE WORKS 139

1315. Fairchild, Hoxie Neal. Religious Trends
in English Poetry. Vol. V: 1880-
1920. Gods of a Changing Poetry.
New York: Columbia University Press,
pp. 85-95, et passim.
1316. Flinn, Fr. Sean, O.F.M. "Scotus and
Hopkins: Christian Metaphysics and
Poetic Creativity," Annual Report of
the Duns Scotus Philosophical Association, XXVI, 50-94.
1317. Gardner, W. H. Correspondence in The
Times Literary Supplement (London),
September 7, p. 673.
1318. Gavin, Sister Rosemarie Julie. "Hopkins'
'The Candle Indoors,'" The Explicator,
XX, No. 6 (February), item 50.
1319. Gomme, A. H. Correspondence in The Times
Literary Supplement (London), April
13, p. 249.
1320. Greiner, Francis J., S.M. "Hopkins'
'The Habit of Perfection,'" The
Explicator, XXI, No. 3 (November),
item 19.
1321. Kernan, Sister M. Noel, S.C. A Critique
of Poetry Compiled From the Prose
Writings of Gerard Manley Hopkins.
Unpublished M.A. thesis, Duquesne
University.
1322. Klapp, Bro. F. "A Closer Look at this
Masterful Work: 'The Blessed Virgin
Mary Compared to the Air We Breathe,'"
The Marianist, LIII, No. 1 (January),
22-25.
1323. Litzinger, Boyd. "Gerard Manley Hopkins,"
The Critic, XXI, No. 2 (October-
November), 36, 39-40.
1324. McNamee, M. B. "Mastery and Mercy in
'The Wreck of the Deutschland,'"
College English, XXIII, No. 4
(January), 267-276.

1325. Myers, John A., Jr. "Intimations of
        Mortality: An Analysis of Hopkins'
        'Spring and Fall,'" The English
        Journal, LI, No. 8 (November), 585-
        587.
1326. Nist, John. "Sound and Sense: Some
        Structures of Poetry," College
        English, XXIII, No. 4 (January),
        291-295.
1327. Norris, Carolyn B. "'Fused Images' in
        the Sermons of Gerard Manley Hopkins,"
        Tennessee Studies in Literature, VII,
        127-133.
1328. Stempel, Daniel. "A Reading of 'The
        Windhover,'" College English, XXIII,
        No. 4 (January), 305-307.
[1222]. Storey, Graham. The Journals and
            Papers of GMH. 1959.
        [1312]. Duncan-Jones, E. E. in The Modern
                    Language Review, LVII, No. 3 (July)
                    431-433.
1329. Templeman, William D. "Ruskin's Plough-
        share and Hopkins' 'The Windhover,'"
        English Studies, XLIII, No. 2 (April),
        103-106.
1330. Westwater, Sister Agnes Martha, S.C.H.
        Sea Imagery in Gerard Manley Hopkins'
        "The Wreck of the Deutschland,"
        Unpublished M.A. thesis, Saint John's
        University.
1331. Woodyard, Vivian Welch. A Study of the
        Vector in the Poetry of Gerard Manley
        Hopkins. Unpublished senior thesis,
        University of California [Riverside].
1332. Wooton, Carl. "The Terrible Fire of
        Gerard Manley Hopkins," Texas Studies
        in Literature and Language, IV, No.
        3 (Autumn), 367-375.

1963

1333. Adams, Juliette Rose Marie. The Theory
of Language in the Poetics of Gerard
Manley Hopkins. Unpublished M.A.
thesis, University of Toronto.
1334. Andreach, Robert Joseph. The Spiritual
Life in Hopkins, Joyce, Eliot, and
Hart Crane. Unpublished Ph.D.
dissertation, New York University.
[In Dissertation Abstracts, XXV, No.
1 (July, 1964), 467.]
1335. Anon. "Fr. G. M. Hopkins in National
Portrait Gallery," Letters and Notices,
LXVIII, No. 330 (March), 5.
1336. August, Eugene R. "Hopkins' Dangerous
Fire," Victorian Poetry, I, No. 1
(January), 72-74.
1337. Bender, Todd K. "Hopkins' 'God's
Grandeur,'" The Explicator, XXI, No.
7 (March), item 55.
1338. Bloom, Lionel. The Mystic Pattern in
the Poetry of Gerard Manley Hopkins.
Unpublished M.A. thesis, Columbia
University.
[1261]. Boyle, Robert. Metaphor in Hopkins.
1961.
1339. Hess, M. Whitcomb. in Spirit, XXX, No.
1 (March), 21-24.
1340. Keating, John E. in Journal of English
and Germanic Philology, LXII, No. 2
(April), 413.
1341. Kreuzer, James R. in Criticism, V, No.
2 (Spring), 191-192.
1342. Rose, E. J. in The Dalhousie Review,
XLIII, No. 1 (Spring), 110-111.
1343. Byrne, Virginia C. "The Creator and
the Maker in the Aesthetics of Gerard
Manley Hopkins," The McNeese Review,
XIV, 60-73.

1344. Campbell, Sister M. Mary Hugh, S.C.M.M.
       "The Silent Sonnet: Hopkins' 'Shep-
       herd's Brow,'" Renascence, XV, No. 3
       (Spring), 133-142.
1345. Chamberlain, Robert L. "George
       MacDonald's 'A Manchester Poem' and
       Hopkin's [sic] 'God's Grandeur,'"
       The Personalist, XLIV, No. 4 (October),
       518-527.
1346. Colavecchio, Barbara Marie. The Domi-
       nant Symbols in Gerard Manley Hopkins'
       "The Wreck of the Deutschland." Un-
       published M.A. thesis, University of
       Rhode Island.
1347. Collins, Winston Lee. Tennyson and
       Hopkins: Intellectual and Poetic
       Affinities. Unpublished M.A. thesis,
       University of Toronto.
1348. D'Angelo, Frank Joseph. "The Wreck of
       the Deutschland" and the Pastoral
       Tradition. Unpublished M.A. thesis,
       Tulane University.
1349. De Souza, Rev. Frederick J. Gerard
       Manley Hopkins: A Closer Look at
       the Terrible Sonnets. Unpublished
       M.A. thesis, Columbia University.
1350. Fike, Francis George, Jr. The Influ-
       ence of John Ruskin upon Aesthetic
       Theory and Practice of Gerard Manley
       Hopkins. Unpublished Ph.D. disser-
       tation, Stanford University.
       [In Dissertation Abstracts, XXV, No.
       2 (August, 1964), 1208.]
1351. Fulweiler, Howard. "Mermen and Mermaids:
       A Note on an Alien Vision in the
       Poetry of Tennyson, Arnold and Hopkins,"
       Victorian Newsletter, No. 23 (Spring),
       pp. 16-17.

1352. Gappa, Richard John. A Critical Evaluation of "The Windhover: To Christ
Our Lord" and its Criticism. Unpublished M.A. thesis, University of
Colorado.

1353. Graves, William L. "Gerard Manley
Hopkins as Composer: An Interpretive
Postscript," Victorian Poetry, I,
No. 2 (April), 146-155.

1354. Greiner, Brother Francis, S.M. "Hopkins'
'The Windhover' Viewed as a Nature
Poem," Renascence, XV, No. 2 (Winter),
68-75, 95.

1355. Grennen, Joseph E. "Grammar as Thauma-
turgy: Hopkins' 'Heraclitean Fire,'"
Renascence, XV, No. 4 (Summer), 208-
211.

1356. Hamilton, Seymour Charles. The Unified
World Vision of Gerard Manley Hopkins.
Unpublished M.A. thesis, University
of Toronto.

1357. Hill, Francis Anthony. An Explication
of "Harry Ploughman" by Gerard Manley
Hopkins as an Inscape of Cosmological
Motion and the Un-moved Mover. Unpublished M.A. thesis, Tulane University.

1358. Hines, Leo. "Pindaric Imagery in G. M.
Hopkins," The Month, n. s., XXIX,
No. 5 (May), 294-307.

1359. Keating, John E. "The Wreck of the
Deutschland": An Essay and Commentary.
(Kent State University Bulletin, Re-
search Series VI, Vol. LI, No. 1.)
Kent, Ohio: Kent State University
Press; 110 pp.

1360. Louise, Sister Robert, O.P. "Hopkins'
       'Spring and Fall: To a Young Child,'"
       The Explicator, XXI, No. 8 (April),
       item 65.
1361. Ludwig, Hans-Werner. Die Self-Komposita
       Bei Thomas Carlyle, Matthew Arnold,
       und Gerard Manley Hopkins: Unter-
       suchungen zum Geistigen Gehalt einer
       Sprachlichen Form. (Studien zur
       Englischen Philologie, n. s., II.)
       Tübinger: Max Niemeyer; 243 pp.
1362. Lukanitsch, Ruth Marion. The Relation-
       ship of the Figures of Sound to the
       Rhythm in Certain Poems of Gerard
       Manley Hopkins. Unpublished Ph.D.
       dissertation, Northwestern University.
       [In Dissertation Abstracts, XXV, No.
       1 (July, 1964), 696.]
1363. McQueen, William A. "'The Windhover'
       and 'St. Alphonsus Rodriguez,'"
       Victorian Newsletter, No. 23 (Spring),
       pp. 25-26.
1364. Masson, David I. "Sound and Sense in a
       Line of Poetry," The British Journal
       of Aesthetics, III, No. 1 (January),
       70-72.
1365. Miller, J. Hillis. The Disappearance
       of God: Five Nineteenth-Century
       Writers. Cambridge, Massachusetts:
       Harvard University Press, pp. 270-
       359, et passim.
1366. Miller, J. Hillis. "The Theme of the
       Disappearance of God in Victorian
       Poetry," Victorian Studies, VI, No. 3
       (March), 207-227.
1367. Milward, Peter, S.J. "The Underthought
       of Shakespeare in Hopkins," Studies
       in English Literature [English Literary
       Society of Japan, University of Tokyo],
       XXXIX, 1-9.

1368. Montag, George E. "Hopkins' 'God's
      Grandeur' and 'The Ooze of Oil
      Crushed,'" Victorian Poetry, I, No.
      4 (November), 302-303.
1369. Norris, Carolyn Brimley. "Gerard Manley
      Hopkins in His Sermons and Poetry,"
      Notes and Queries, n. s., X, No. 1
      (January), 27.
1370. Ochshorn, Myron Gustav. Hopkins the
      Critic: The Literary Judgment and
      Taste of Gerard Manley Hopkins, with
      an Appendix of His Verse Theory.
      Edited with Notes and an Introduction.
      Unpublished Ph.D. dissertation, Uni-
      versity of New Mexico.
      [In Dissertation Abstracts, XXV, No.
      6 (December, 1964), 3579-3580.]
1371. Olney, James Leslie. George Herbert and
      Gerard Manley Hopkins: A Comparative
      Study in Two Religious Poets. Unpub-
      lished Ph.D. dissertation, Columbia
      University.
      [In Dissertation Abstracts, XXV, No.
      3 (September, 1964), 1895-1896.]
1372. Pouncey, Lorene. Gerard Manley Hopkins'
      Sextet of "Terrible Sonnets": An
      Analytical Study. Unpublished M.A.
      thesis, University of Houston.
1373. Riley, Sister Maria Amabilis. A Compa-
      rative Study Showing the Influence of
      John Keats on Gerard Manley Hopkins.
      Unpublished M.A. thesis, Florida
      State University.
1374. Ritz, Jean-Georges. Le Poète Gérard
      Manley Hopkins, S.J. (1844-1889): Sa
      vie et son Oeuvre. Paris: Didier;
      726 pp.

1375. Singh, Yashoda N. "Gerard Manley
       Hopkins: A Problem of Prosody," An
       English Miscellany [St. Stephen's
       College, Delhi, India], No. 2, pp.
       49-56.
1376. Smith, Grover. "A Source for Hopkins'
       'Spring and Fall' in The Mill on The
       Floss?" English Language Notes, I,
       No. 1 (September), 43-46.
1377. Stenton, Cathryn Davis. A Study of the
       Poetic Theories of Coventry Patmore,
       Robert Bridges, and Gerard Hopkins
       as the Basis for a System of Modern
       Prosody. Unpublished M.A. thesis,
       University of Nebraska.
1378. Stevens, Sister Mary Dominic, O.P.
       "Hopkins' 'That Nature Is a Heraclitean
       Fire,'" The Explicator, XXII, No. 3
       (November), item 18.
1379. Townsend, Gerard James. A Comparative
       Study of "The Wreck of the Deutsch-
       land" by Gerard Manley Hopkins and
       "The Dark Night of the Soul" by St.
       John of the Cross. Unpublished M.A.
       thesis, Tulane University.
1380. Wills, Mary Suzanne. An Analysis of
       the Influence of the Spiritual Exer-
       cises of St. Ignatius on the Poetry
       of Gerard Manley Hopkins. Unpub-
       lished M.A. thesis, Indiana State
       University.

                    1964
1381. Agnew, Francis Henry, C.M. The Poetic
       Theory of Gerard Manley Hopkins and
       The Philosophy of Duns Scotus. Un-
       published M.A. thesis, DePaul
       University.

1382. Andreach, Robert J. Studies in
        Structure. New York: Fordham Uni-
        versity Press, pp. 12-39, et passim.
1383. August, Eugene Robert. Word Inscapes:
        A Study of the Poetic Vocabulary of
        Gerard Manley Hopkins. Unpublished
        Ph.D. dissertation, University of
        Pittsburgh.
        [In Dissertation Abstracts, XXVI,
        No. 6 (December, 1965), 3294-3295.]
1384. Augusta, Sister Paul, O.P. A Commentary
        on the "Terrible Sonnets" of Gerard
        Manley Hopkins. Unpublished M.A.
        thesis, University of New Mexico.
1385. Bates, Ronald. "Hopkins' Embers Poems:
        A Liturgical Source," Renascence,
        XVII, No. 1 (Fall), 32-37.
1386. Bates, Ronald. "'The Windhover,'"
        Victorian Poetry, II, No. 1 (Winter),
        63-64.
1387. Brown, Marie Patricia. The Sensuous
        Concept of Nature in G. M. Hopkins'
        Poetic Images. Unpublished M.A.
        thesis, Georgetown University.
1388. Colson, Ted Donald. An Analysis of
        Selected Poems of Gerard Manley
        Hopkins for Oral Interpretation and
        a Study of His Poetic Theories. Un-
        published Ph.D. dissertation, Univer-
        sity of Oklahoma.
        [In Dissertation Abstracts, XXIV, No.
        12 (June), 5604.]
1389. Dilligan, Robert. An Abstract of the
        Influence of John Keats on Gerard
        Manley Hopkins. Unpublished M.A.
        Thesis, Columbia University.

1390. Doherty, Francis. "A Note on 'Spelt
       from Sibyl's Leaves,'" Essays in
       Criticism, XIV, No. 4 (October),
       428-432.
[1193]. Downes, David A. GMH: A Study of His
       Ignatian Spriit. 1959.
       1391. Pick, John. in Renascence, XVI, No. 3
              (Spring), 163-165.
1392. Giovannini, Giovanni. "A Literal Gloss
       of Hopkins' 'The Windhover,'" in
       Linguistic and Literary Studies in
       Honor of Helmut A. Hatzfeld, ed.
       Alessandro S. Crisafulli. Washington,
       D. C.:   The Catholic University of
       America Press, pp. 203-212.
1393. Gomme, Andor. "A Note on Two Hopkins
       Sonnets," Essays in Criticism, XIV,
       No. 3 (July), 327-331.
1394. Haas, Charles Eugene. A Structural
       Analysis of Selected Sonnets of
       Gerard Manley Hopkins. Unpublished
       Ph.D. dissertation, University of
       Denver.
       [In Dissertation Abstracts, XXV, No.
       9 (March, 1965), 5443.]
1395. Hafley, James. "Hopkins: 'A Little
       Sickness in the Air,'" The Arizona
       Quarterly, XX, No. 3 (Fall), 215-222.
1396. Herring, Mary Lynn. Gerard Manley
       Hopkins as a Critic of Poetry. Un-
       published M.A. thesis, University of
       Tennessee.
1397. Huntley, John F. "Hopkins' 'The Wind-
       hover' as a Prayer of Request,"
       Renascence, XVI, No. 3 (Spring), 154-
       162.
[1359]. Keating, John E.   "The Wreck of the
       Deutschland." 1963.

1398. Boyle, Robert, S.J. in Journal of
      English Philology, LXIII, No. 3
      (July), 536-538.
1399. Kopper, Edward A., Jr. "Hopkins' 'The
      Windhover,'" The Explicator, XXII,
      No. 7 (March), item 54.
1400. Litzinger, Boyd. "The Pattern of Ascent
      in Hopkins," Victorian Poetry, II,
      No. 1 (Winter), 43-47.
1401. Marx, Carola Maxine. Gerard Manley
      Hopkins: "Spring and Fall: To A
      Young Child"--A Study of Poetic
      Compression. Unpublished M.A. thesis,
      Cornell University.
1402. McNamara, Peter L. "Motivation and
      Meaning in the 'Terrible Sonnets,'"
      Renascence, XVI, No. 2 (Winter), 78-
      80, 94.
1403. Miller, Bruce E. "On 'The Windhover,'"
      Victorian Poetry, II, No. 2 (Spring),
      115-119.
1404. Murray, Neil A. The Prosodic Theory and
      Practice of Patmore, Hopkins, and
      Bridges. Unpublished M.A. thesis,
      Memorial University of Newfoundland.
1405. Nielson, Sister Ancilla of the Immaculate,
      D.W. The Scotist Element in Hopkins.
      Unpublished M.A. thesis, Saint John's
      University.
1406. Noel, Sister Mary, S.C. "Gathering to
      a Greatness: A Study of 'God's
      Grandeur,'" English Journal, LIII,
      No. 4 (April), 285-287.
1407. Olson, Signe. "Meaning and Obscurity--
      Gerard Manley Hopkins," Discourse,
      VII, No. 2 (Spring), 188-200.

150   GERARD MANLEY HOPKINS

1408. Orr, Paul A. The Artistic Principles of
       Gerard Manley Hopkins. Unpublished
       Ph.D. dissertation, University of
       Notre Dame.
       [In Dissertation Abstracts, XXV, No.
       5 (November), 2965-2966.]
1409. Pendexter, Hugh, III. "Hopkins' 'God's
       Grandeur,'" The Explicator, XXIII,
       No. 1 (September), item 2.
1410. Prosen, Anthony J., S.J. "Suffering in
       Aeschylus and Hopkins," The Classical
       Bulletin, XLI, No. 1 (November), 11-
       13.
1411. Rader, Louis. Major Problems in Hopkins
       Criticism. Unpublished Ph.D. disser-
       tation, Cornell University.
1412. Shea, F. X., S.J. "Another Look at 'The
       Windhover,'" Victorian Poetry, II,
       No 4 (Autumn), 219-239.
1413. Tripp, Kathryn Stewart. Gerard Manley
       Hopkins and the Self. Unpublished
       M.A. thesis, Columbia University.
1414. Watson, Thomas L. "Hopkins 'God's
       Grandeur,'" The Explicator, XXII, No.
       6 (February), item 47.

                    1965
1415. Abbott, William Henry. The Image in the
       Poetry of Gerard Manley Hopkins.
       Unpublished M.A. thesis, Louisiana
       State University.
1416. Anon. "An Uncollected Letter of Gerard
       Manley Hopkins," The Dublin Review,
       CCXXXIX, No. 505 (Autumn), 289-292.
1417. Camp, Burr A. Gerard Manley Hopkins'
       Sonnets of Desolation: An Analysis
       of the Qualitative Sound Structure.
       Unpublished thesis, Barry College.

1418. Cattaui, Georges. "Gérard Manley Hopkins et 'l'inspect' des choses," Critique [Paris], XXI, No. 222 (November), 935-949.

1419. Chard, Leslie F., II. "Once More into 'The Windhover,'" English Language Notes, II, No. 4 (June), 282-285.

1420. Chevigny, Bell Gale. "Instress and Devotion in the Poetry of Gerard Manley Hopkins," Victorian Studies, IX, No. 2 (December), 141-153.

1421. Clark, Robert Boykin. "Hopkins's 'The Shepherd's Brow,'" Victorian Newsletter, No. 28 (Fall), pp. 16-18.

1422. Cooper, Benjamin Evans. Vertical Movement in the Poetry of Gerard Manley Hopkins: An Insight to the Poet's Thought. Unpublished M.A. thesis, University of Virginia.

1423. Delahunty, Kenneth R. Guilt and the Grail: Hopkins, Poet in the Active Voice; Wakefield, Mon Frère. Unpublished M.A. thesis, Pennsylvania State University.

1424. Downes, David A. "Hopkins and Thomism," Victorian Poetry, III, No. 4 (Autumn), 270-272.

1425. Downes, David Anthony. Victorian Portraits: Hopkins and Pater. New York: Bookman Associates, Inc.; 176 pp.

        1426. Pick, John. in Renascence, XVIII, No. 1 (Autumn), 53.

1427. Driscoll, John P. "Hopkins' 'Spring,' line 2, and 'Spring and Fall: To a Young Child,' line 2," The Explicator, XXIV, No. 3 (November), item 26.

1428. Fiore, Amadeus. "Hopkins' Relation to the Deutschland Nuns," Renascence, XVIII, No. 1 (Autumn), 45-48.

1429. Giovannini, Margaret. "Hopkins' 'God's
      Grandeur,'" The Explicator, XXIV, No.
      4 (December), item 36.
1430. Hart, Lucia Carolina Romberg. The Poetry
      of Gerard Manley Hopkins. Unpublished
      M.A. thesis, University of Texas.
1431. Honora, Sister, D.C. "Positively Speak-
      ing: Gerard Manley Hopkins," Delta
      Epsilon Sigma Bulletin, X, No. 3
      (October), 69-77.
1432. Houle, Sister Mary John Bosco, B.V.M.
      "Readings of Two Victorian Poems,"
      Iowa English Yearbook, No. 10 (Fall),
      pp. 50-52.
      [Meredith's "The Lark Ascending" and
      Hopkins' "The Caged Skylark."]
1433. Johnson, Ronald W. Gerard Manley
      Hopkins: His Approach to Literary
      Criticism. Unpublished M.A. thesis,
      Colorado State University.
[1359]. Keating, John E. "The Wreck of the
      Deutschland." 1963.
      1434. Lees, F. N. in Notes and Queries, n.
            s., XII, No. 2 (February), 74-75.
1435. Lovas, John Charles. The Poet and his
      God: A Study of the Religious Verse
      of Gerard Manley Hopkins. Unpub-
      lished M.A. thesis, University of
      Utah.
1436. MacKenzie, Norman H. Correspondence
      in The Times Literary Supplement
      (London), March 18, p. 220.
      [On Hopkins manuscripts.]
1437. MacKenzie, Norman H. "Gerard and Grace
      Hopkins: Some New Links," The Month,
      n.s., XXXIII, No. 6 (June), 347-350.

1438. Marsh, Derick. "Part, Pen, Pack: A
       Critical Reading of Two Poems by G.
       M. Hopkins," Balcony: The Sydney
       Review, No. 2 (Winter), pp. 19-27.
1439. Mellown, Elgin W. "The Reception of
       Gerard Manley Hopkins' Poems, 1918-
       1930," Modern Philology, LXIII, No.
       1 (August), 38-51.
1440. Montag, George E. "'The Windhover':
       Crucifixion and Redemption," Victo-
       rian Poetry, III, No. 2 (Spring),
       109-118.
1441. Nassar, Eugene. "Hopkins, Figura, and
       Grace: God's Better Beauty," Renas-
       cence, XVII, No. 3 (Spring), 128-130,136.
1442. Ochshorn, Myron. "Hopkins the Critic,"
       The Yale Review, LIV, No. 3 (Spring),
       346-367.
1443. Pace, George B. "On the Octave Rhymes
       of 'The Windhover,'" English Language
       Notes, II, No. 4 (June), 285-286.
1444. Pitts, Arthur W., Jr. "Hopkins' 'The
       Wreck of the Deutschland,' Stanza
       29," The Explicator, XXIV, No. 1
       (September), item 7.
1445. Schneider, Elisabeth W. "Sprung Rhythm:
       A Chapter in the Evolution of Nine-
       teenth-Century Verse," Publications
       of the Modern Language Association
       of America, LXXX, No. 3 (June), 237-
       253.
1446. Talbot, Norman. "A Note on 'God's
       Grandeur,'" Balcony: The Sydney Re-
       view, No. 3 (Spring), p. 46.
1447. Thomas, A., S.J. "G. M. Hopkins and the
       Silver Jubilee Album," The Library,
       5th ser., XX, No. 2 (June), 148-152.

1448. Thomas, A. "G. M. Hopkins and 'Tones,'"
       Notes and Queries, n. s., XII, No. 11
       (November), 429-430.
1449. Thomas, A., S.J. "A Note on Gerard
       Manley Hopkins and his Superiors
       1868-77," The Irish Ecclesiastical
       Record, 5th ser., CIV (October-
       November), 286-291.
1450. Towner, Annemarie Ewing. "Welsh Bardic
       Meters and English Poetry," The
       Massachusetts Review, VI, No. 3
       (Spring-Summer), 614-624.
1451. Yetzer, Bernard Edward. The Victorianism
       of Gerard Manley Hopkins. Unpublished
       M.A. thesis, University of Oklahoma.

                          1966
1452. Barton, John M. T. Correspondence in
       The Times Literary Supplement (London),
       October 20, p. 959.
1453. Bender, Todd K. Gerard Manley Hopkins:
       The Classical Background and Critical
       Reception of His Work. Baltimore,
       Maryland: The Johns Hopkins Press;
       viii, 172 pp.
1454. Chamberlain, Charles Martin, III.
       Hopkins' Rejection of Aestheticism.
       Unpublished Ph.D. dissertation,
       University of Colorado.
       [In Dissertation Abstracts, XXVIII,
       No. 2(August, 1967), 620-621-A.]
1455. De Graaff, Robert Mark. Scotism in the
       Poetry of Gerard Manley Hopkins.
       Unpublished M.A. thesis, Miami Uni-
       versity [Oxford, Ohio].
[1425]. Downes, David Anthony. Victorian Por-
       traits: Hopkins and Pater. 1965.
         1456. DeLaura, David J. in Victorian Studies,
                IX, No. 3 (March), 282-283.

1457. Driskell, Leon V. "The Progressive
      Structure of 'The Windhover,'"
      Renascence, XIX, No. 1 (Autumn), 30-
      36.
1458. Dumbleton, William A. The Literary
      Relationship of Robert Bridges to
      Gerard Manley Hopkins, 1889-1930.
      Unpublished Ph.D. dissertation, Uni-
      versity of Pennsylvania.
      [In Dissertation Abstracts, XXVIII,
      No. 1 (July, 1967), 227A.]
1459. Franz, Louis Joseph. The Concept of the
      "Mystical Body of Christ" in Selected
      Poems of Gerard Manley Hopkins. Un-
      published Ph.D. dissertation, Univer-
      sity of Southern California.
      [In Dissertation Abstracts, XXVII,
      No. 9 (March, 1967), 3045-A.]
1460. Fulweiler, Howard W. "Gerard Manley
      Hopkins and the 'Stanching, Quenching
      Ocean of a Motionable Mind,'" Vic-
      torian Newsletter, No. 30 (Fall),
      pp. 6-13.
1461. Gardner, W. H. Correspondence in The
      Times Literary Supplement (London),
      September 15, p. 868.
      [Reply to Vickers, in TLS, March 3;
      on Hopkins and Newman.]
1462. Gold, R[aymond]. Notes on Poetry and
      Prose of Gerard Manley Hopkins.
      Bath, Somerset: James Brodie Ltd.:
      72 pp.
1463. Hartman, Geoffrey H., ed. Hopkins: A
      Collection of Critical Essays.
      (Twentieth Century Views, No. 57.)
      Englewood Cliffs, New Jersey:
      Prentice-Hall, Inc.; viii, 182 pp.
      Bridges, Robert. "The Oddities of
      Genius," 71-75.

Burkhardt, Sigurd. "Poetry and the Lan-
guage of Communion," 160-167.
Guardini, Romano. "Aesthetic-Theological
Thoughts on 'The Windhover,'" 76-79.
Hartman, Geoffrey H. "The Dialectic of
Sense-Perception," 117-130.
Hartman, Geoffrey H. "Introduction:
Poetry and Justification," 1-16.
Leavis, F. R. "Gerard Manley Hopkins,"
17-36.
Matthiessen, F. O. "Hopkins and Whitman,"
144-150.
McLuhan, Herbert Marshall. "The Analog-
ical Mirrors," 80-88.
Melchiori, Giorgio. "Two Mannerists:
James and Hopkins," 131-143.
Miller, J. Hillis. "The Univocal
Chiming," 89-116.
Ong, Walter J. "Sprung Rhythm and
English Tradition," 151-159.
Wain, John. "An Idiom of Desperation,"
57-70.
Warren, Austin. "Instress of Inscape,"
168-177.
Winters, Yvor. "Gerard Manley Hopkins,"
37-56.
1464. Hill, Archibald A. "'The Windhover'
Revisited: Linguistic Analysis of
Poetry Reassessed," Texas Studies in
Literature and Language, VII, No. 4
(Winter), 349-359.
1465. Hufstader, Dom Anselm. "The Experience
of Nature in Hopkins' Journal and
Poems," The Downside Review, LXXXIV,
No. 275 (April), 127-149.
1466. Hunter, Jim. Gerard Manley Hopkins.
(Literature in Perspective.) London:
Evans Brothers Limited; 160 pp.

CRITICISM OF THE WORKS   157

1467. Kenneally, John Daniel. The Personal
       and Literary Relationship of Gerard
       Manley Hopkins and Richard Watson
       Dixon. Unpublished Ph.D. disser-
       tation, Fordham University.
       [In Dissertation Abstracts, XXVII,
       No. 2 (August), 458.]
1468. King, Donald R. "The Vision of 'Being'
       in Hopkins' Poetry and Ruskin's
       'Modern Painters' I," Discourse, IX,
       No. 3 (Summer), 316-324.
1469. Klotz, Rose Mosen. Verbal Counterpoint
       in the Poetry of Gerard Manley Hopkins.
       Unpublished Ph.D. dissertation, Uni-
       versity of Wisconsin.
       [In Dissertation Abstracts, XXVII,
       No. 4 (October), 1058-1059.]
1470. Lees, Francis Noel. Gerard Manley
       Hopkins. (Columbia Essays on Modern
       Writers, No. 21.) New York & London:
       Columbia University Press; 48 pp.
1471. MacKenzie, Norman H. Correspondence in
       The Times Literary Supplement (London),
       February 10, p. 110.
       [Reply to Thomas, in TLS, January 20.]
1472. O'Dea, Richard J. "'The Loss of the
       Eurydice': A Possible Key to the
       Reading of Hopkins," Victorian Poetry,
       IV, No. 4 (Autumn), 291-293.
1473. Pick, John. A Hopkins Reader. Revised
       and enlarged edition. Garden City,
       New York: Image Books; 439 pp.
1474. Reiman, Donald H. "Hopkins' 'Ooze of
       Oil' Rises Again," Victorian Poetry,
       IV, No. 1 (Winter), 39-42.
1475. Schneider, Elisabeth W. "'The Wreck of
       the Deutschland': A New Reading,"
       Publications of the Modern Language
       Association of America, LXXXI, No. 1
       (March), 110-122.

1476. Sharples, Sister Marian, I.H.M. "Con-
      jecturing a Date for Hopkins' 'St.
      Thecla,'" Victorian Poetry, IV, No.
      3 (Summer), 204-209.
1477. Stein, Karen F. Hopkins' The Wreck of
      The Deutschland: An Aesthetic
      Analysis. Unpublished M.A. thesis,
      Pennsylvania State University.
1478. Thomas, Alfred, S.J. Correspondence in
      The Times Literary Supplement (Lon-
      don), January 20, p. 48.
      [On a misplaced fragmentary letter
      from Hopkins to his mother, dated
      January 28, 1877.]
1479. Thomas, Alfred, S.J. Correspondence in
      The Times Literary Supplement (Lon-
      don), October 27, p. 981.
      [On the rejection of "The Wreck of
      the Deutschland" by The Month.]
1480. Thomas, A. "G. M. Hopkins: An Unpub-
      lished Triolet," The Modern Language
      Review, LXI, No. 2 (April), 183-187.
1481. Thomas, Alfred, S.J. "Gerard Manley
      Hopkins: Doomed to Success by
      Failure," The Dublin Review, CCXL,
      No. 508 (Summer), 161-175.
1482. Vickers, Brian. Correspondence in The
      Times Literary Supplement (London),
      March 3, p. 178.
      [On Hopkins and Newman.]
1483. Walker, Alan. The Influence of Welsh
      Poetry on That of Gerard Manley
      Hopkins and Dylan Thomas. Unpub-
      lished M.A. thesis, University of
      Toronto.
1484. White, Gertrude M. "Hopkins' 'God's
      Grandeur': A Poetic Statement of
      Christian Doctrine," Victorian Poetry,
      IV, No. 4 (Autumn), 284-287.

1485. Winter, J. L. "Notes on 'The Windhover,'"
       Victorian Poetry, IV, No. 3 (Summer),
       212-213.

                       1967
1486. August, Eugene R. "The Growth of 'The
       Windhover,'" Publications of the
       Modern Language Association of
       America, LXXXII, No. 5 (October),
       465-468.
1487. Badin, Donatella A. "L'Epistolario di
       Gerard Manley Hopkins," in Studi e
       ricerche di letteratura inglese e
       americana (No. 1), ed. Agostino
       Lombardo. Milan: Editoriale
       Cisalpino, pp. 221-272.
1488. Bates, Ronald. "Downdolphinry," Uni-
       versity of Toronto Quarterly, XXXVI,
       No. 3 (April), 229-236.
[1453]. Bender, Todd K. Gerard Manley Hopkins:
       The Classical Background and
       Critical Reception of His Work.
       1966.
       1489. Boyle, Robert, S.J. in Journal of
              English and Germanic Philology, LXVI,
              No. 4 (October), 609-613.
       1490. Boyle, Robert, S.J. in Thought, XLII,
              No. 167 (Winter), 624-626.
       1491. MacKenzie, Norman H. in Queen's
              Quarterly, LXXIV, No. 3 (Autumn),
              547-548.
1492. Blythe, Harold Russell. Hopkins' "The
       Wreck of the Deutschland": A Critical
       Study. Unpublished M.A. thesis,
       University of Florida.
1493. Cohen, Edward H. "A Comprehensive
       Hopkins Bibliography: 1863-1918,"
       Bulletin of Bibliography, XXV, No. 4
       (September-December), 79-81.

1494. Cohen, Edward H. A Bibliography In-
       cluding the Published Works of Gerard
       Manley Hopkins and Criticism of the
       Works of Gerard Manley Hopkins. Un-
       published Ph.D. dissertation, Univer-
       sity of New Mexico.
1495. Doherty, Paul C. "Hopkins' 'Spring and
       Fall: To a Young Child,'" Vic-
       torian Poetry, V, No. 2 (Summer),
       140-143.
1496. Elkins, Bill James. Hopkins' Terrible
       Sonnets: A Study of the Poetic Pro-
       gression. Unpublished Ph.D. disser-
       tation, Ohio University.
       [In Dissertation Abstracts, XXVII,
       No. 12 (June), 4219A.]
1497. Fraser, Ronald. "'The Windhover' Again,"
       The Downside Review, LXXXV, 71-73.
1498. Füger, Wilhelm. "Gerard Manley Hopkins
       am Werk: Zum Entstehungsprozess von
       'The Starlight Night,'" Di Neuren
       Sprachen, LXVI, No. 9 (September),
       428-439.
1499. Gardner, W. H. Correspondence in The
       Times Literary Supplement (London),
       August 3, p. 707.
       [On Poems of Gerard Manley Hopkins,
       4th ed.]
1500. Gardner, W. H., and N. H. Mackenzie.
       "Introduction," The Poems of Gerard
       Manley Hopkins. Fourth edition.
       London and New York: Oxford Univer-
       sity Press, pp. i-lxvii.
   1501. Anon. in The Times Literary Supplement
          (London), October 5, p. 937.
   1502. Burgess, Anthony. in Spectator,
          September 22, pp. 326-327.
   1503. Levi, Peter, S.J. in Manchester Guard-
          ian Weekly, September 14, p. 11.

1504. Maccaig, Norman. in The Listener,
       LXXVIII (October 26), 545.
1505. Gibson, Frances. "The Influence of
       Welsh Prosody on the Poetry of
       Hopkins," Xavier University Studies
       [New Orleans, Louisiana], VI, No. 1
       (February), 21-28.
1506. Hallgarth, Susan A. "A Study of Hopkins'
       Use of Nature," Victorian Poetry, V,
       No. 2 (Summer), 79-92.
[1463]. Hartman, Geoffrey H. Hopkins: A
       Collection of Critical Essays.
       1966.
   1507. Nist, John. in Western Humanities Re-
          view, XXI, No. 1 (Winter), 72-73.
1508. Jankowsky, Kurt R. Die Versauffassung
       bei Gerard Manley Hopkins, den
       Imagisten und T. S. Eliot. Munich:
       Max Hueber Verlag; 339 pp.
[1470]. Lees, Francis Noel. Gerard Manley
       Hopkins. 1966.
   1509. Maxwell, J. C. in Notes and Queries,
          n. s., XIV, No. 10 (October), 398-399.
1510. Litzinger, Boyd. "Once More, 'The Wind-
       hover,'" Victorian Poetry, V, No. 3
       (Autumn), 228-230.
1511. McLaughlin, John, S.J. The Pulpit
       Rhetoric of Gerard Manley Hopkins.
       Unpublished Ph.D. dissertation,
       Columbia University.
       [In Dissertation Abstracts, XXVIII,
       No. 2 (August), 770A.]
1512. Mariani, Paul L. "Hopkins' 'Felix
       Randall' As Sacramental Vision,"
       Renascence, XIX, No. 4 (Summer), 217-
       220.

1513. Müller-Schwefe, Gerhard. "Gerard Manley
       Hopkins: 'Spelt from Sibyl's Leaves,'"
       in Die moderne englische Lyrik:
       Interpretationen, ed. Horst Oppel.
       Berlin: Erich Schmidt Verlag, pp.
       39-48.
1514. Ong, Walter J. "Evolution, Myth and
       Poetic Vision," In the Human Grain:
       Further Explorations of Contemporary
       Culture. New York: The Macmillan
       Company, pp. 99-126.
       [On "The Wreck of the Deutschland."]
1515. Payne, Michael. "Syntactical Analysis
       and 'The Windhover,'" Renascence,
       XIX, No. 2 (Winter), 88-92.
1516. Pendergrass, Paula Belcher. The Dark
       Sonnets of Gerard Manley Hopkins:
       A Critical Study. Unpublished M.A.
       thesis, University of Florida.
1517. Prendeville, Brendan. "Visible Thought,"
       The British Journal of Aesthetics,
       VII, No. 4 (October), 339-349.
       [Compares Hopkins' concept of inscape
       with modern aesthetic and psycholog-
       ical theories.]
1518. Rader, Louis. "Hopkins' Dark Sonnets:
       Another New Expression," Victorian
       Poetry, V, No. 1 (Spring), 13-20.
1519. Sharples, Sister Marian, I.H.M. "Hopkins
       and Joyce: A Point of Similarity,"
       Renascence, XIX, No. 3 (Spring),
       156-160.
1520. Sonstroem, David. "Making Earnest of
       Game: G. M. Hopkins and Nonsense
       Poetry," Modern Language Quarterly,
       XXVIII, No. 2 (June), 192-206.
1521. Storey, Graham. "Introduction," Hopkins
       Selections. London: Oxford Univer-
       sity Press, p. i-vii.

[1501]. Anon. in The Times Literary Supple-
          ment (London), October 5, p. 937.
[1503]. Levi, Peter, S.J. in Manchester
          Guardian Weekly, September 14,
          p. 11.
1522. Taylor, Michael. "Hopkins' 'God's
          Grandeur,' 3-4", The Explicator,
          XXV, No. 8 (April), item 68.

INDEX

INDEX TO CRITICS

167

Bell, Sr. Ann Charles, S.N.D.   1175

Bender, Todd Kay   1303, 1337,
1453

Benét, William Rose   174, 523

Berchmans, Sr. Louise, S.N.D.   286

Bernad, Miguel A., S.M.   1304

Bernstein, Melvin Herbert   434

Berryman, John   498

Bett, Henry   799

Bewley, Marius   812

Binsse, H. L.   90

Binyon, Laurence   393

Birrell, T. A.   1111

Bischoff, Dolph Anthony, S.J.   524, 579, 821,
890, 910, 1032,
1112, 1122,
1151, 1185

Blackmur, R. P.   300, 388

Bliss, Geoffrey   525

Bloom, Lionel   1338

Blum, Sr. Magdalen Louise, S.C.   844

Blume, Bernhard   1176

Blythe, Harold R.   1492

Boas, Frederic   6

Bogan, Louise   346, 1033

Boner, Harold A.   127

Bonn, John Louis, S.J.   819

Bowen, Robert O.   1034, 1177

Boyle, Robert R., S.J.   526, 527, 755, 819, 1035, 1123, 1235, 1261, 1398, 1489, 1490

Bradbrook, M. C.   1019

Brauns, M., S.J.   608

Brégy, Katherine   12, 14, 16, 394

Bremond, André, S.J.   161, 241, 415, 609

Brennan, Joseph Xavier   756

Brennan, Norman Charles   1310

Bretelle, Leon   1085

Bridges, Robert   7, 8, 28, 1463

Brinlee, Robert Washington   1152

186

Guardini, Romano	1271, 1463
Guidi, Augusto	641, 675, 676, 873, 919, 1054
Guiney, Louise Imogen	41, 42, 43
Gutiérrez Mora, José Manuel	862, 920, 1007
Guzie, Tad W., S.J.	1130
Gwynn, Frederick L.	897
H., R. B.	584
Haas, Charles Eugene	1394
Haas, Willy	1055
Hache, M. Irene Marie, R.C.E.	784
Haddakin, Lilian	715
Hafley, James	1395
Hallgarth, Susan A.	1506
Halsband, Robert	831, 972
Hamilton, Seymour Charles	1356
Hanlon, R. W.	503
Hansen-Löve, Friedrich	921
Hanson, W. G.	553
Harding, H. W.	554

Hone, J. M.	27
Honora, Sr. D. C.	1431
Hope, Felix	109
Hopkins, Gerard	555
Hopkins, J. G. E.	504
Hopkins, L. C.	231
Horst, Karl August	1059
Hough, Graham	1080
Houle, Sr. Mary J. Bosco, B.V.M.	1432
House, Humphry	143, 241, 296, 556, 788
Howarth, R. G.	621, 678, 679, 716, 865, 1205
Hufstader, Dom Anselm	1465
Hughes, Emily	375, 409, 557
Hughes, Riley	585
Humiliata, Sr. Mary	1060
Hunter, Jim	1466
Huntley, John F.	1397
James, Stanley B.	232, 269, 376
Jankowsky, Kurt R.	1093, 1508

Pick, John	362, 381, 427, 459, 470, 492, 517, 568, 589, 616, 650, 662, 707, 711, 775, 776, 804, 814, 858, 960, 1021, 1081, 1099, 1119, 1191, 1201, 1202, 1391, 1426, 1473
Pickman, Hester	96
Pietrkiewicz, Jerzy	732
Pinto, Vivian de Sola	901, 1069, 1252
Pitchford, Lois W.	935
Pitts, Arthur W., Jr.	1444
Plomer, William	151
Plowman, Max	244, 245.
Plures	59
Pocs, John A.	1290
Pompen, Fr. Aurelius, O.F.M.	332
Porter, Alan	67
Pouncey, Lorene	1372
Prendeville, Brendan	1517

Price, Fanny 570

Price, R. G. G. 777

Prosen, Anthony J., S.J. 1410

Pryce-Jones, Alan 116

Purcell, J. M. 686

Putnam, Sam 68

Quinn, Kerker 363

R., M. R. 179

Rader, Louis 1291, 1411,
1518

Rathmell, J. C. A. 1215

Ratliff, John D. 1142

Raymond, William O. 902

Read, Herbert 113, 136, 153,
154, 214, 236,
277, 382, 989

Reeves, James 903, 980, 990,
1253

Reid, J. C. 571, 1254

Reiman, Donald H. 1474

Retinger, Sr. Mary Anthony 904

Richards, I. A. 72, 73, 80